The Luton Auguries

Timothy

Prus

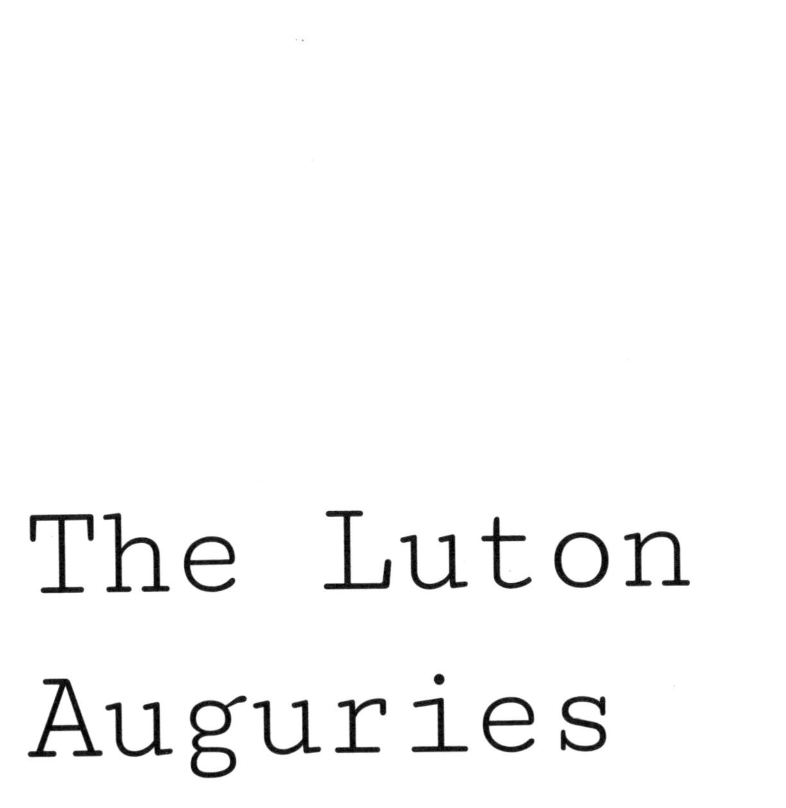
The Luton
Auguries

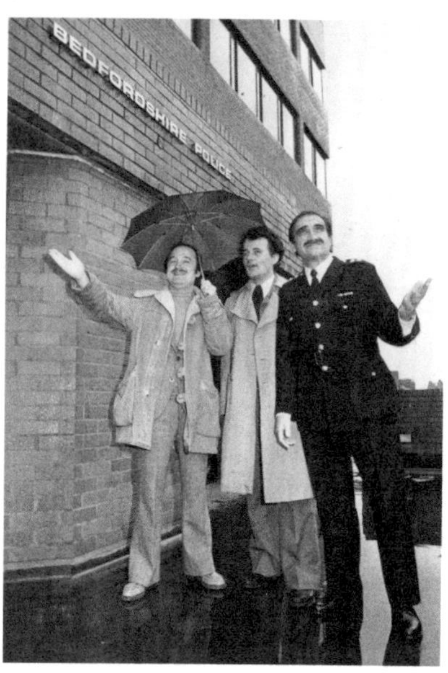

French police inspectors Jean Valat and Andre Seigneur come to Luton and examine the phenomena.

Water diviner Ernest Clear searches for holy water.

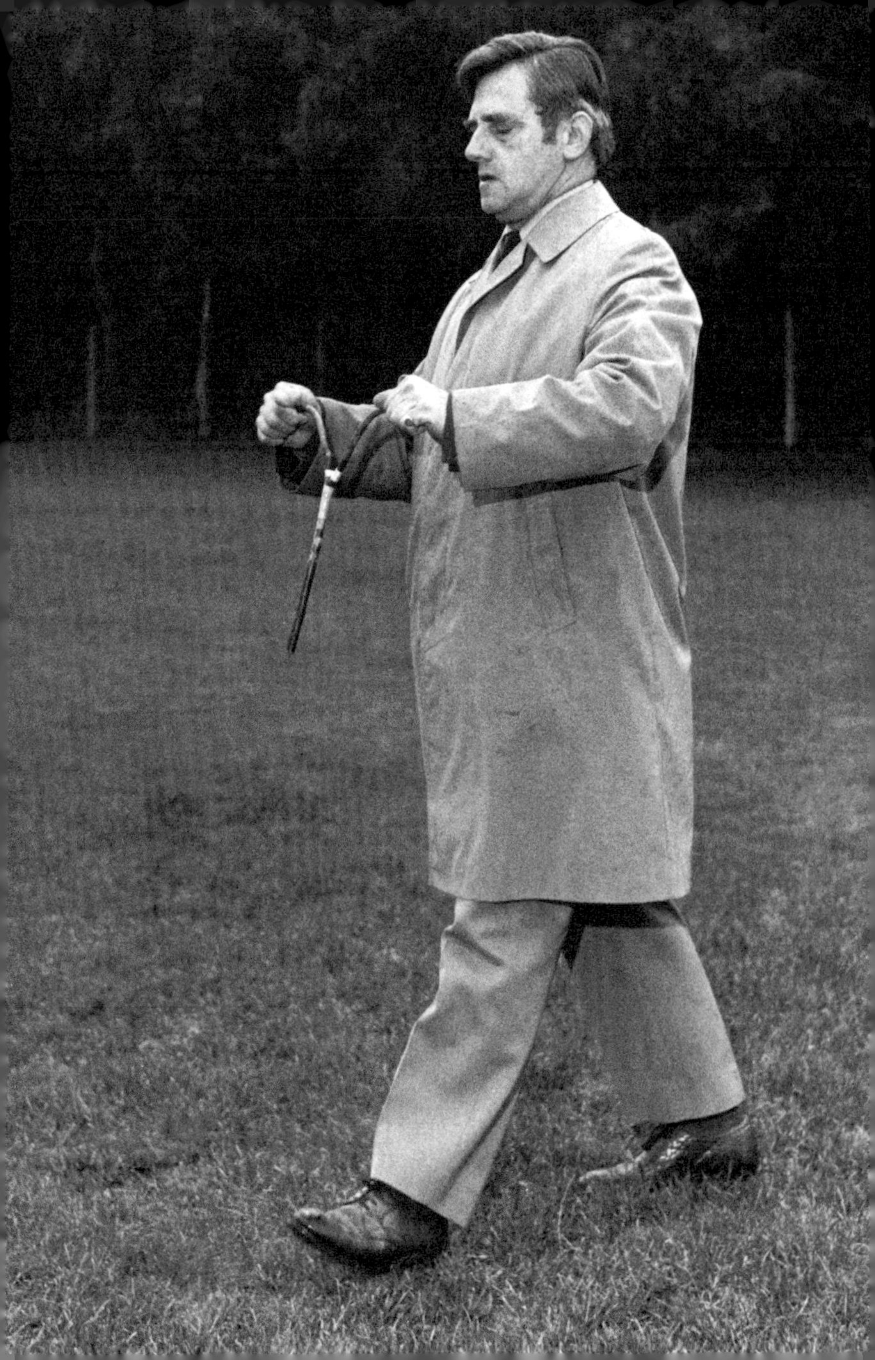

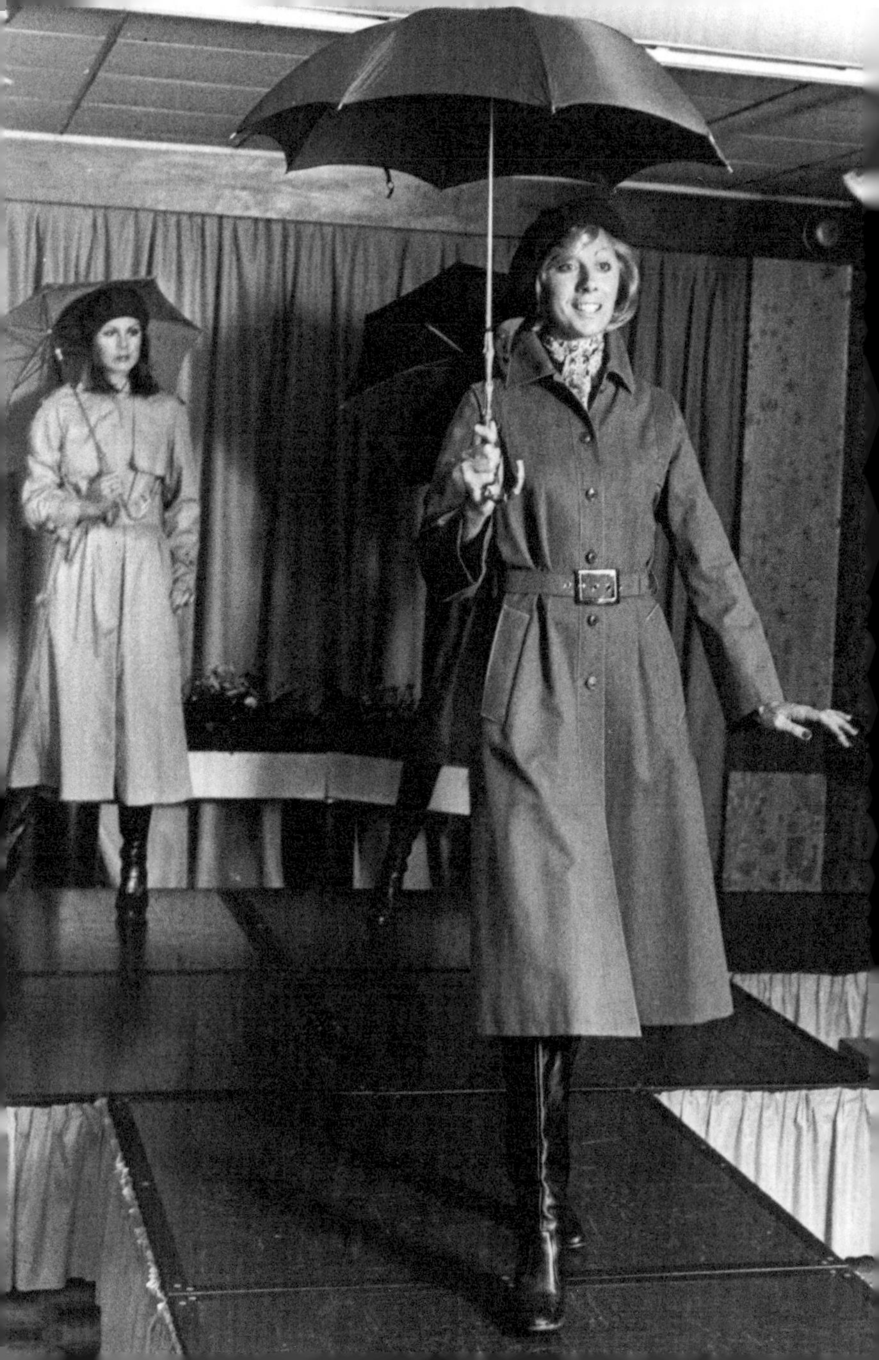

Look chic when it rains inside.

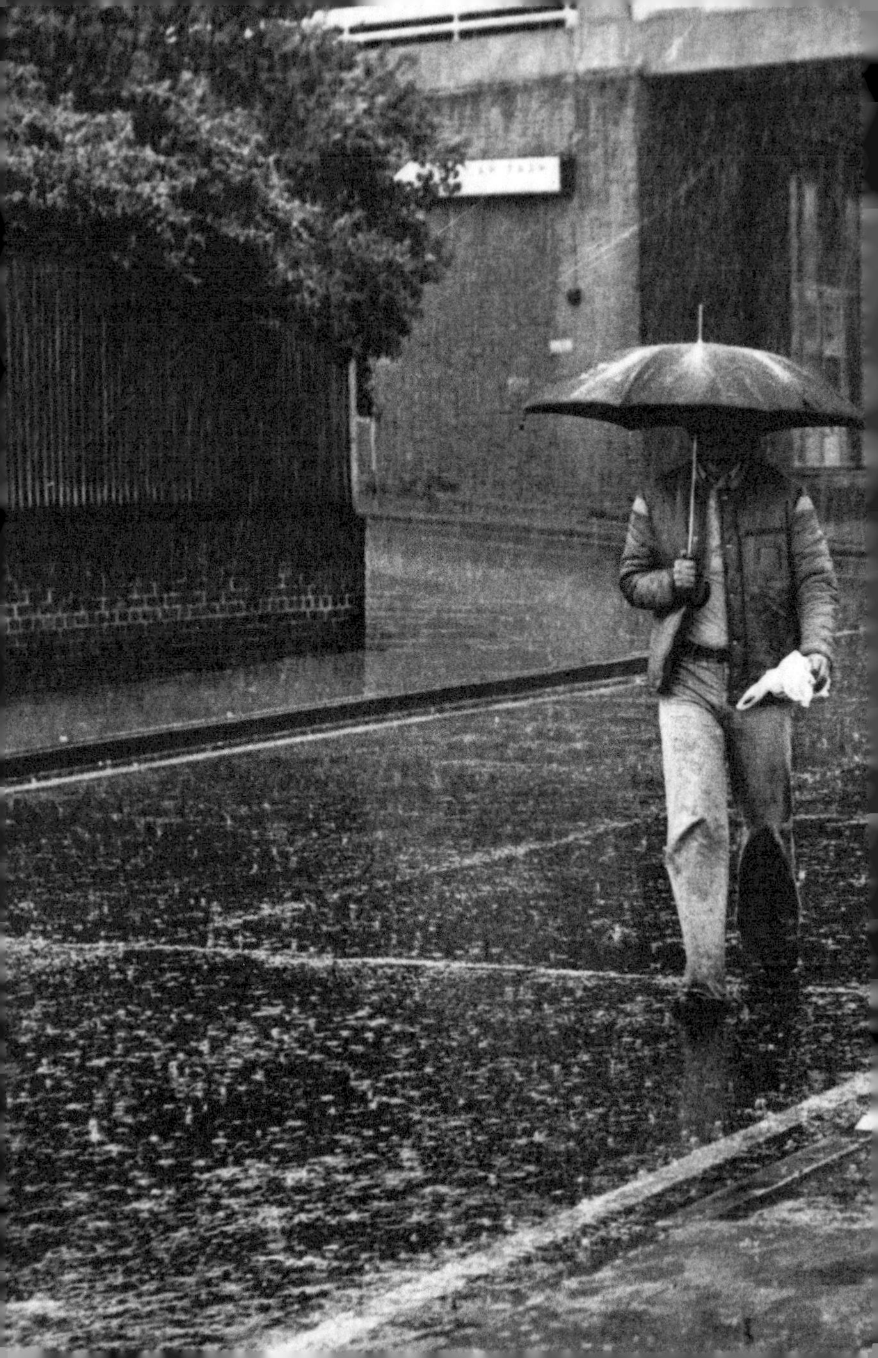

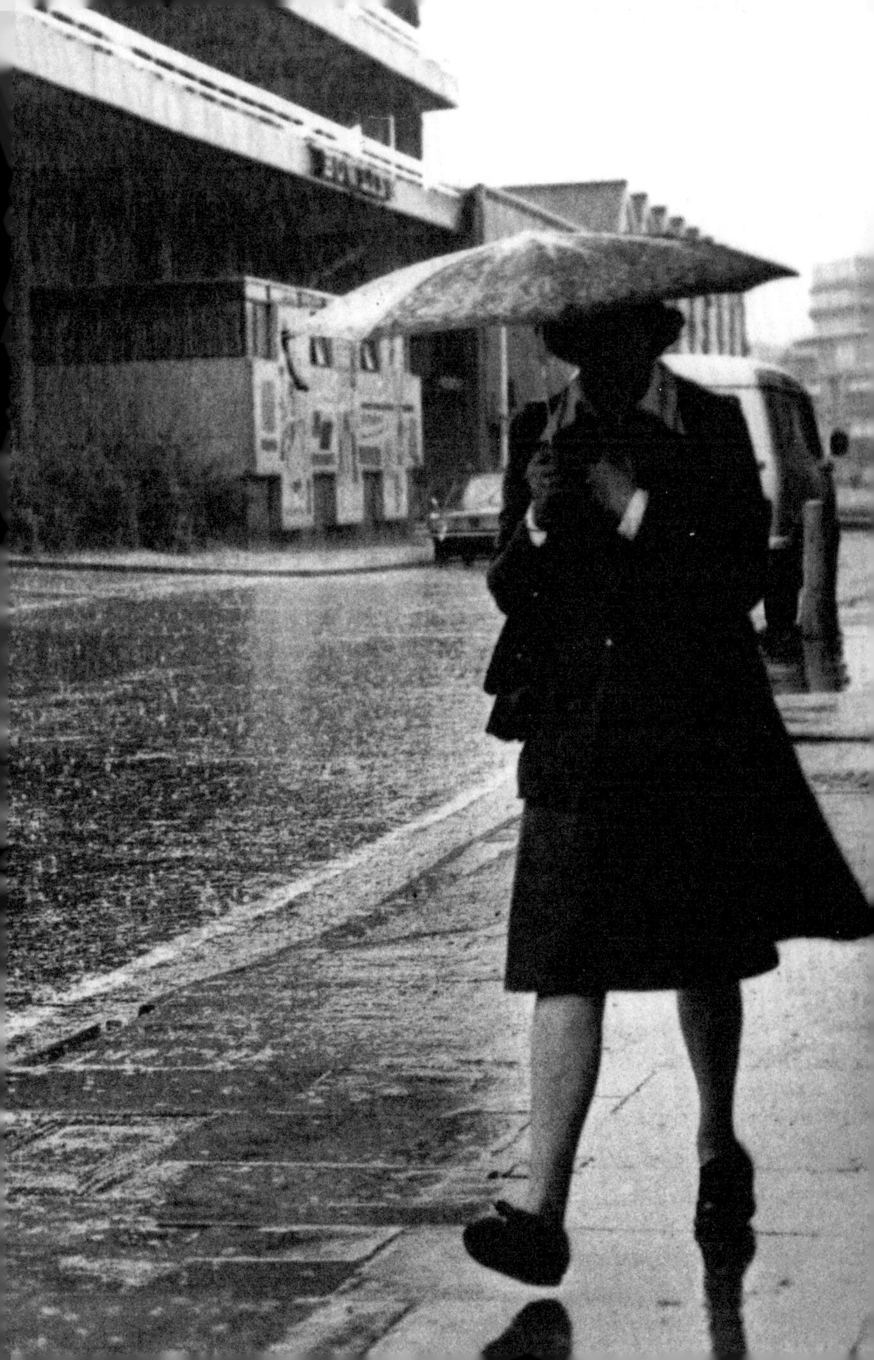

The most persistent rains since records began.

Luton hit hard by continuous rains.

Indoor sunshine at a cosmetic recreation suite.

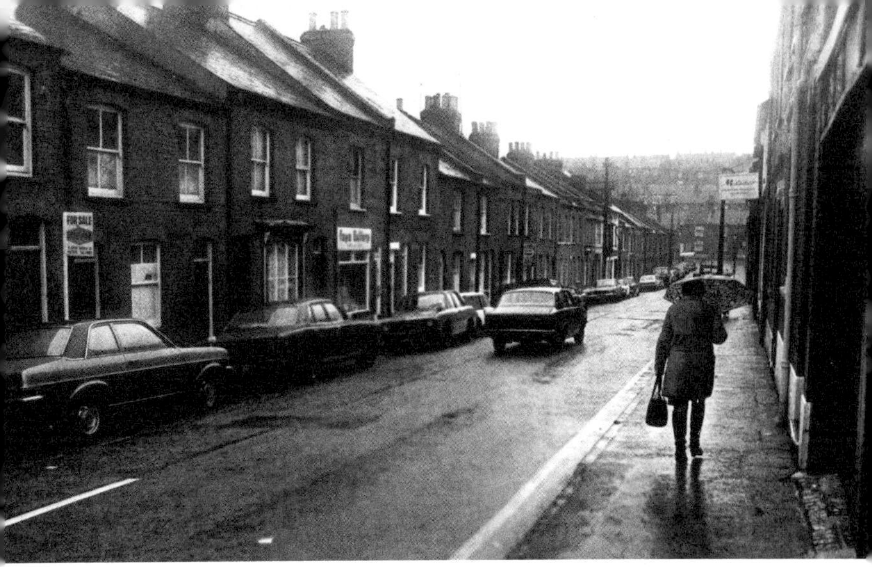

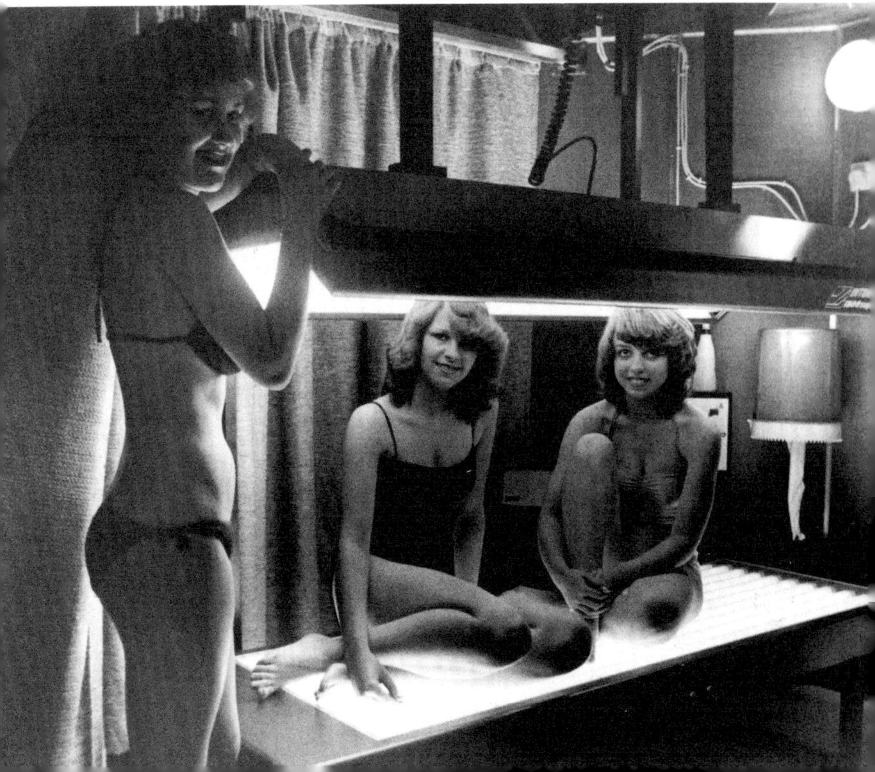

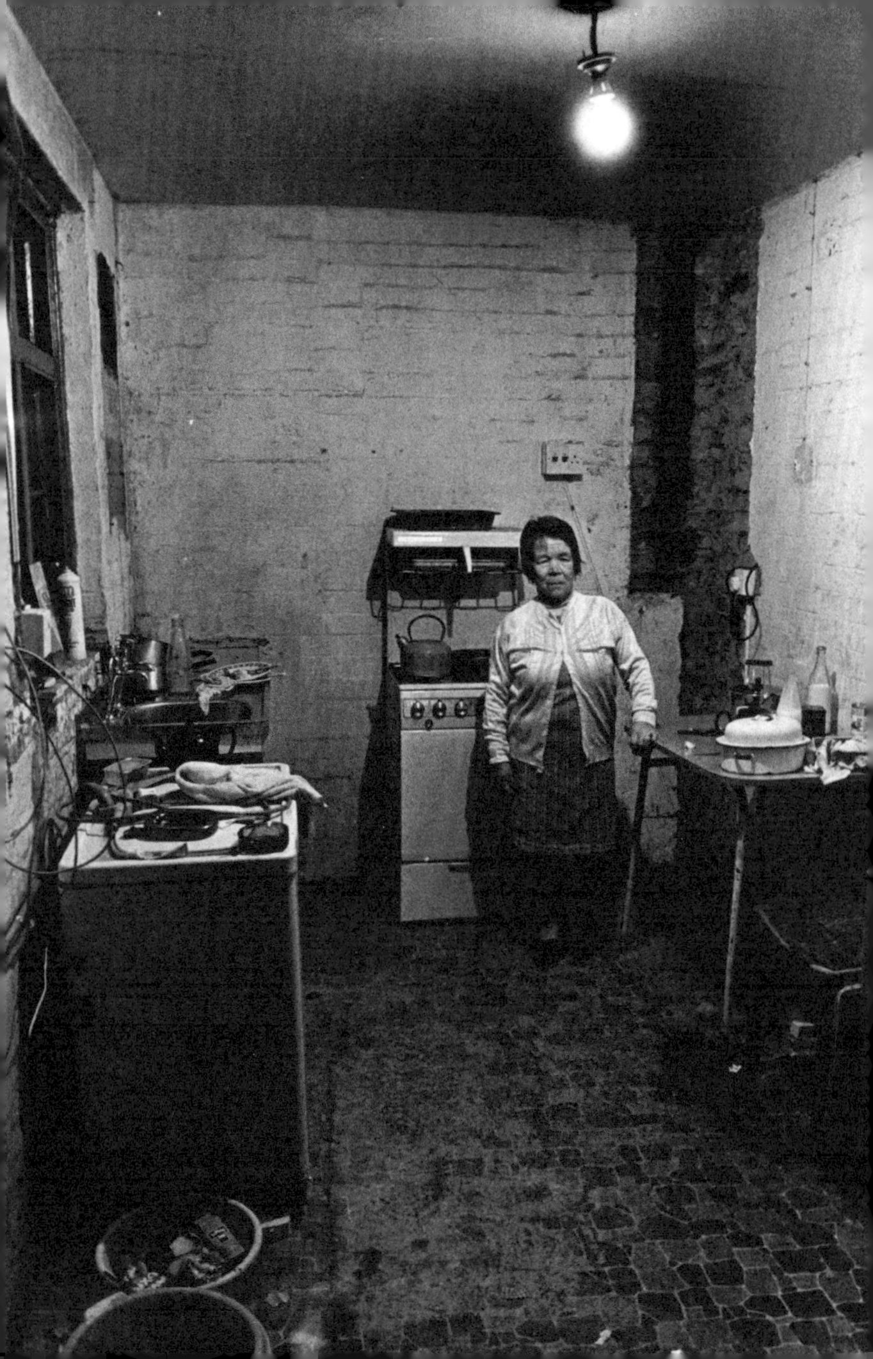

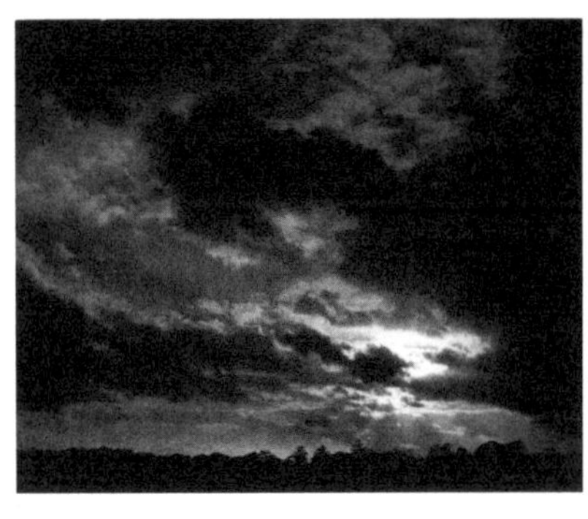

The clouds continue to roll in.

Damp permeates the kitchen.

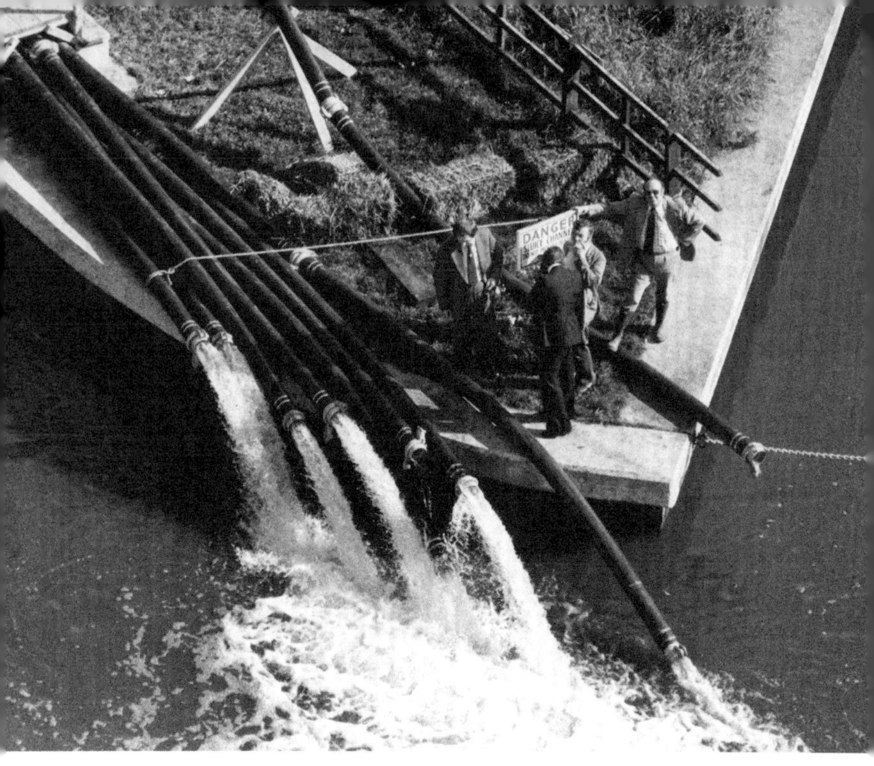

Sluice channels are constructed.

It is too late for some residents in Napier Road. Their walls have been declared damp beyond repair. They will be demolished.

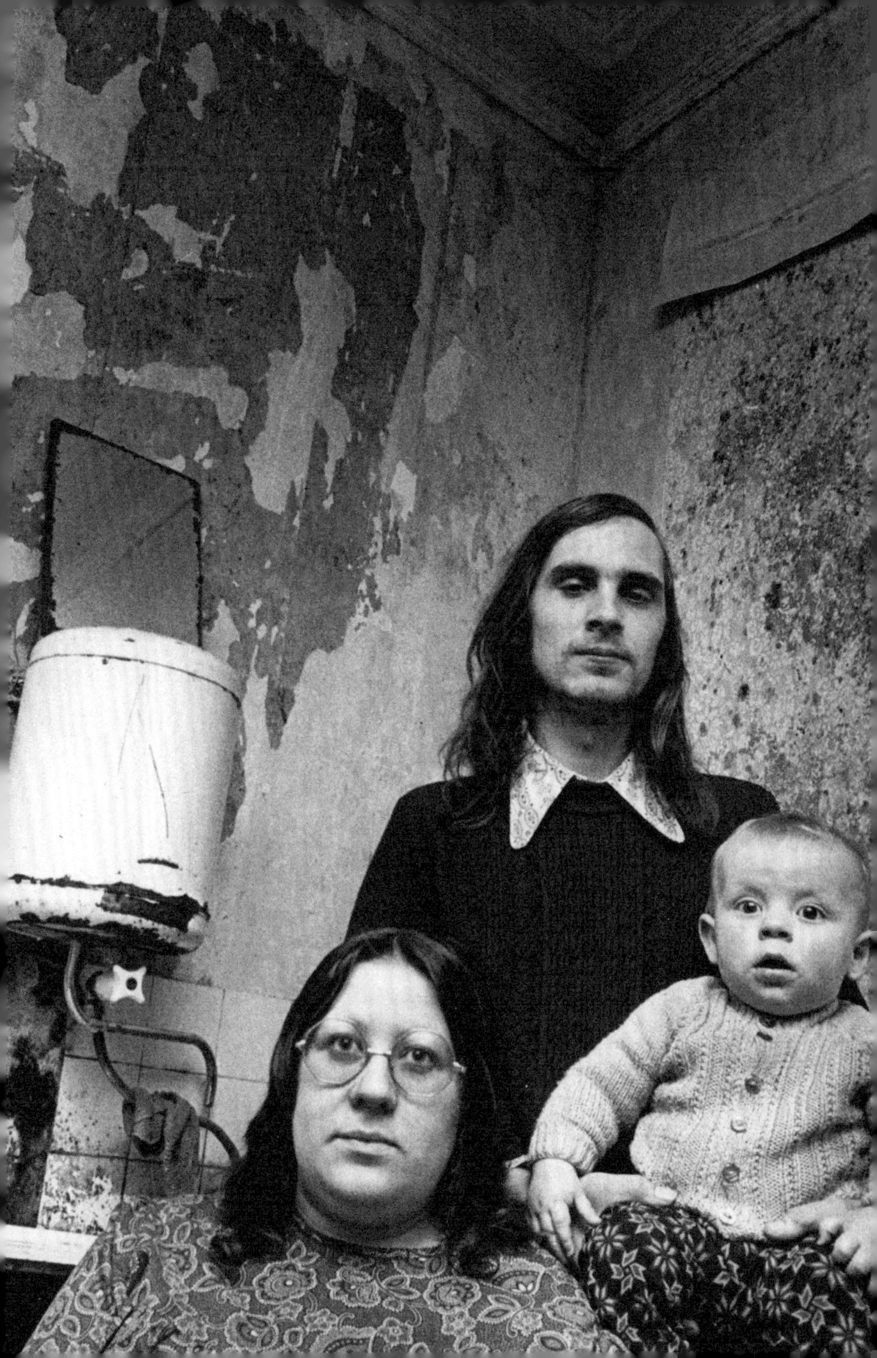

The landscape has been transformed in Bucks, Beds and Herts.

At High Town it's getting into their bones.
Coats are never taken off.

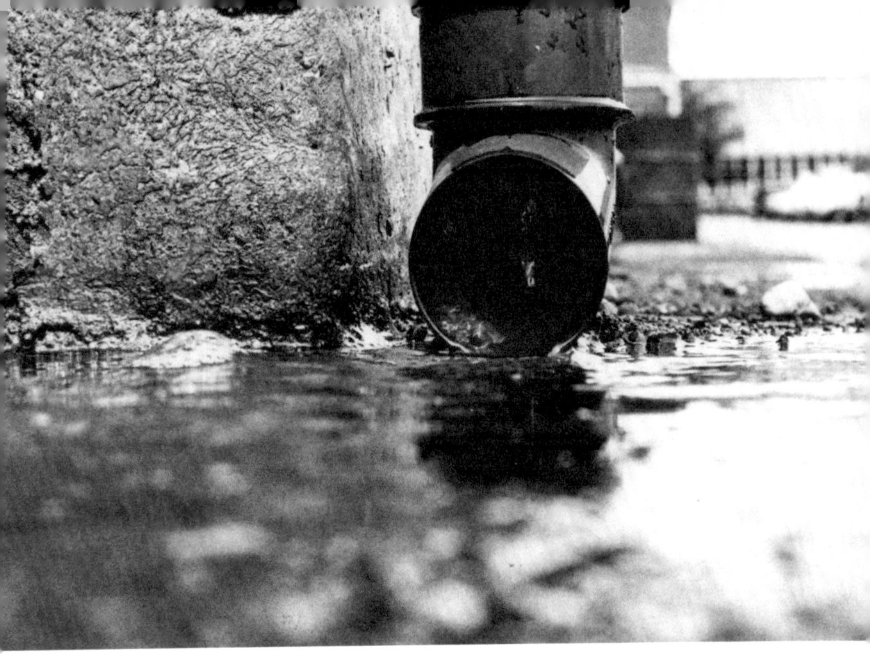

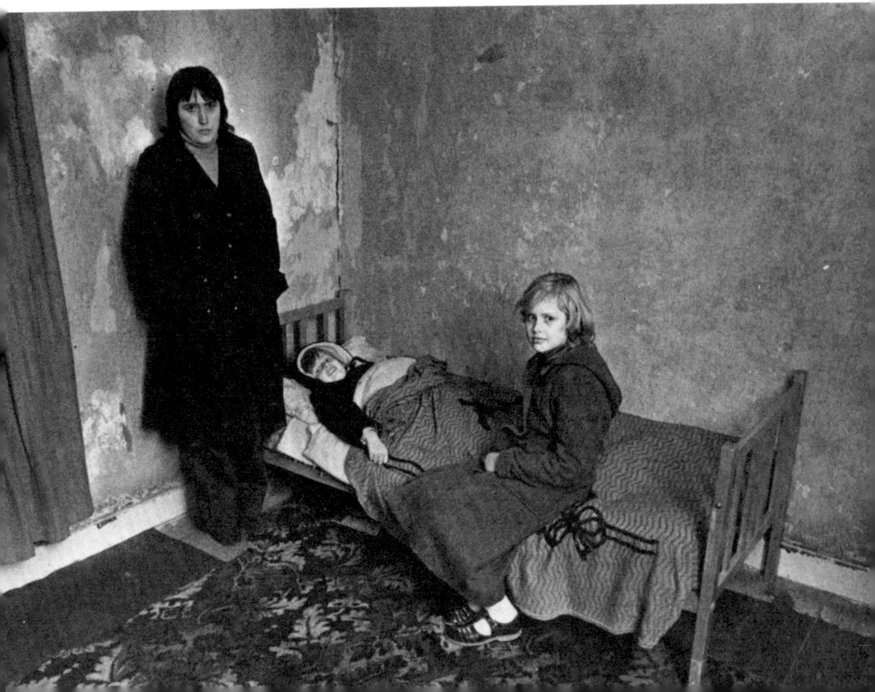

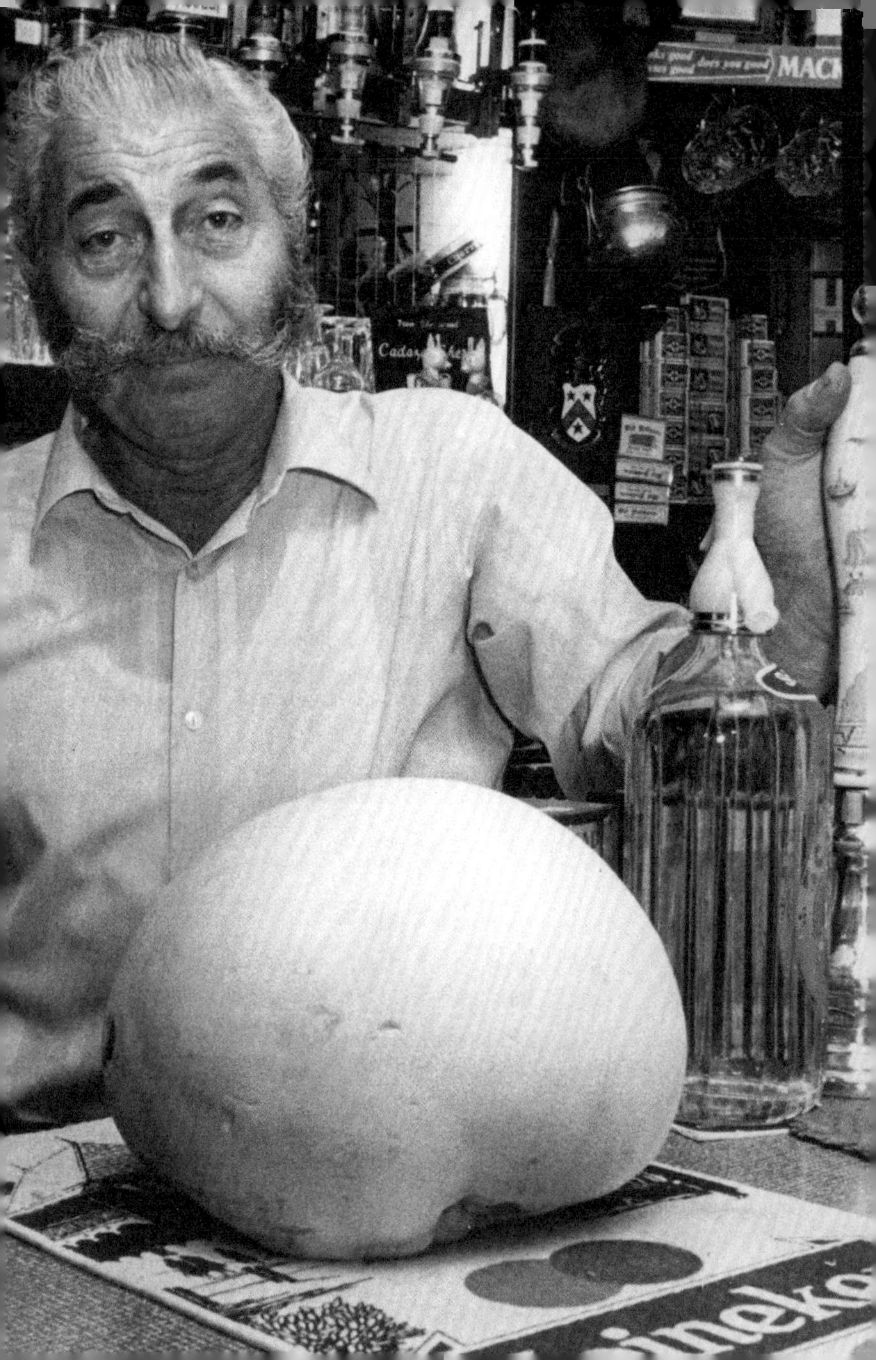

At the Rose and Crown, regulars are stunned by the giant puffballs growing in the bar as well as in the street outside. Representatives from Rothamsted experimental station have attended the scene.

Full baptisms have become a feature on the River Bourne.

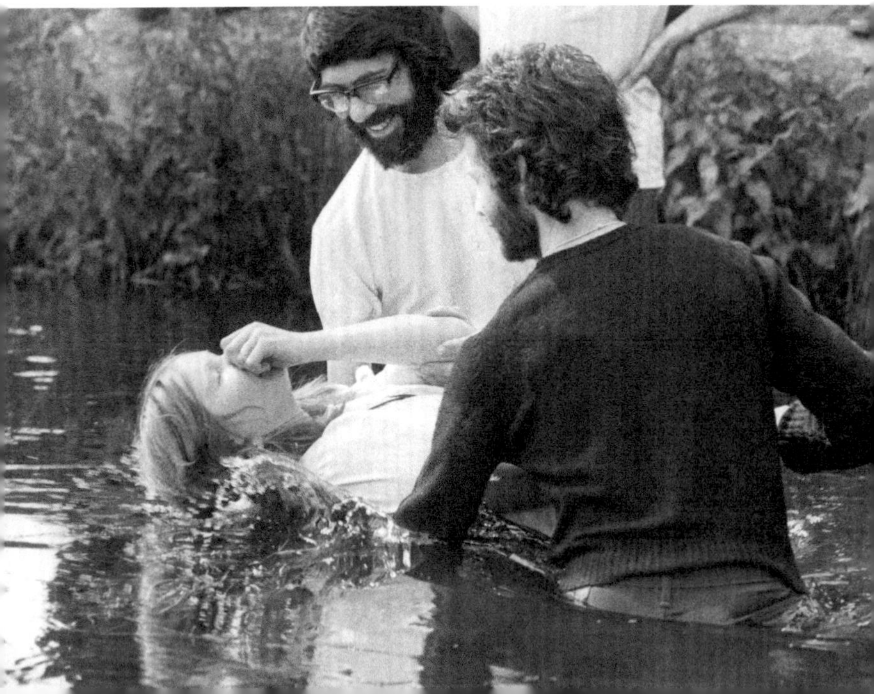

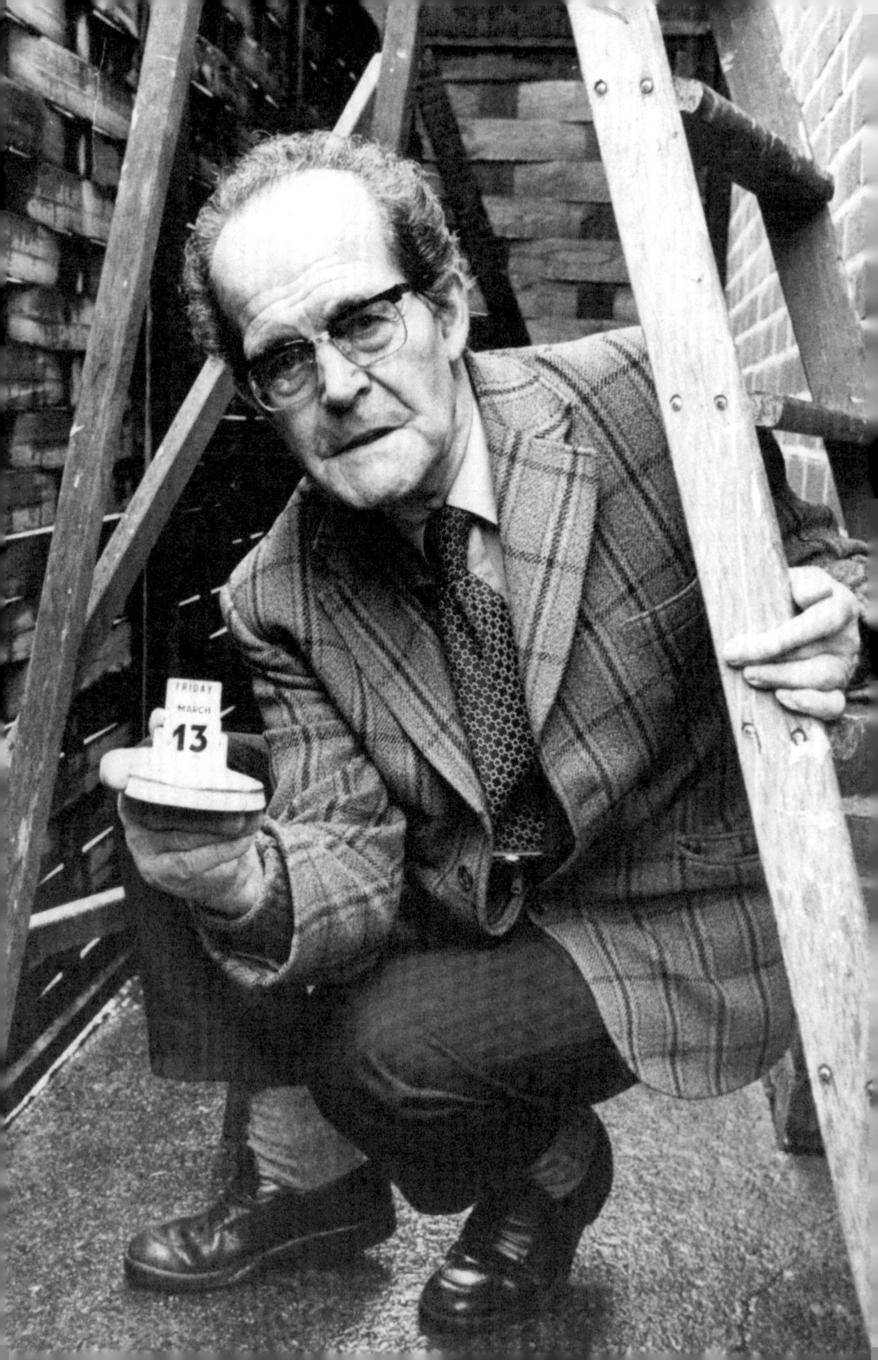
FRIDAY
MARCH
13

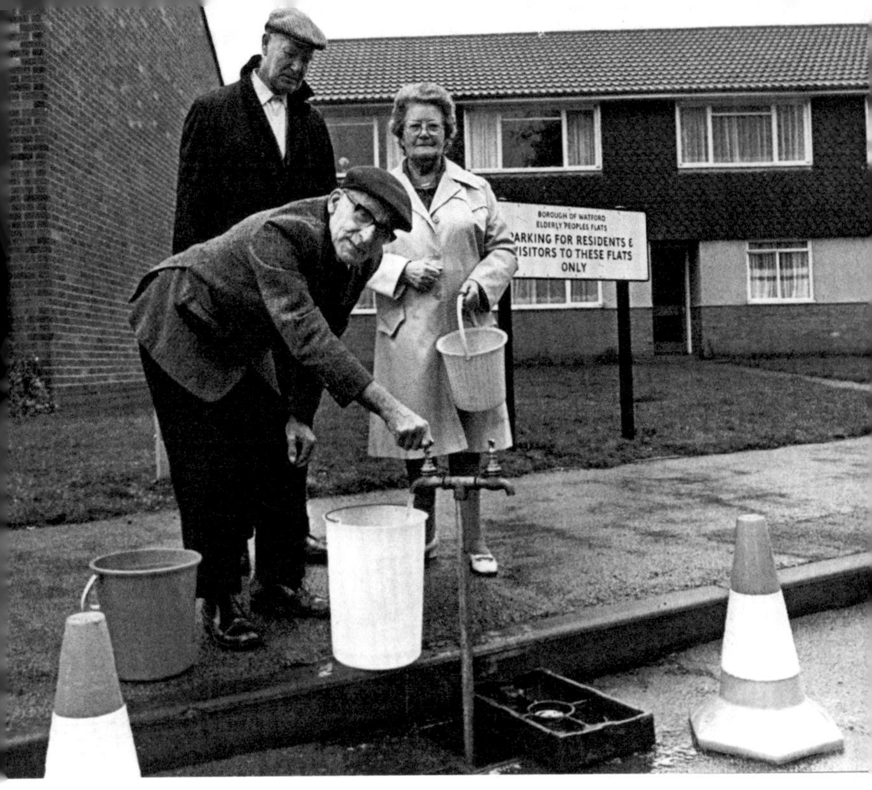

The water supply has been seriously affected by the current weather conditions. Standpipes have become a mainstay.

Old superstitions are being revived.

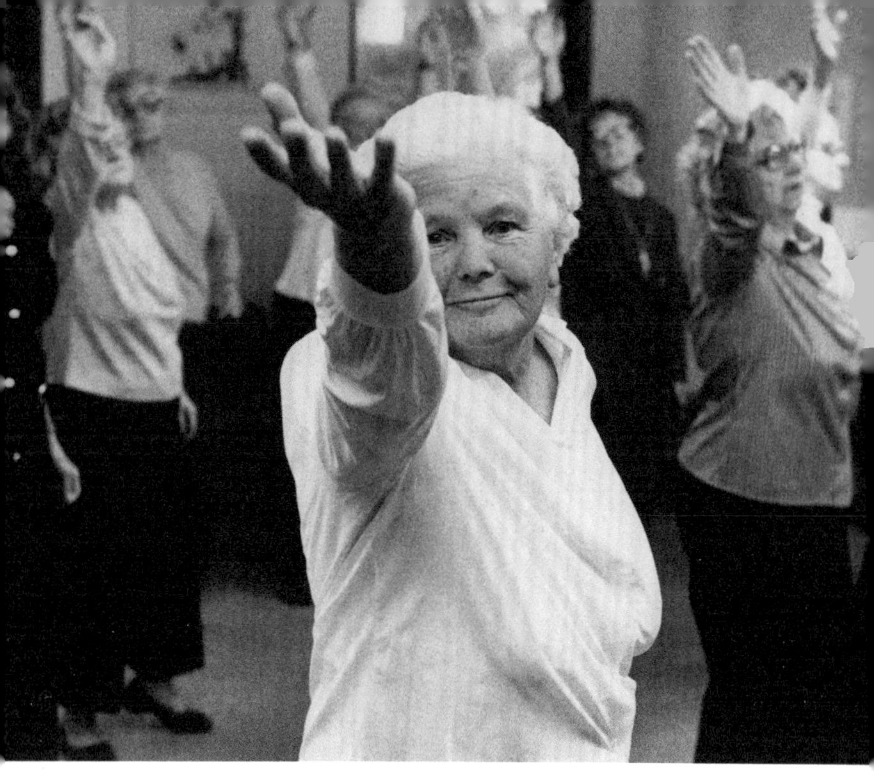

Prayers are offered in Houghton Regis.

A giant chalice for the rains has been built at Baydon.

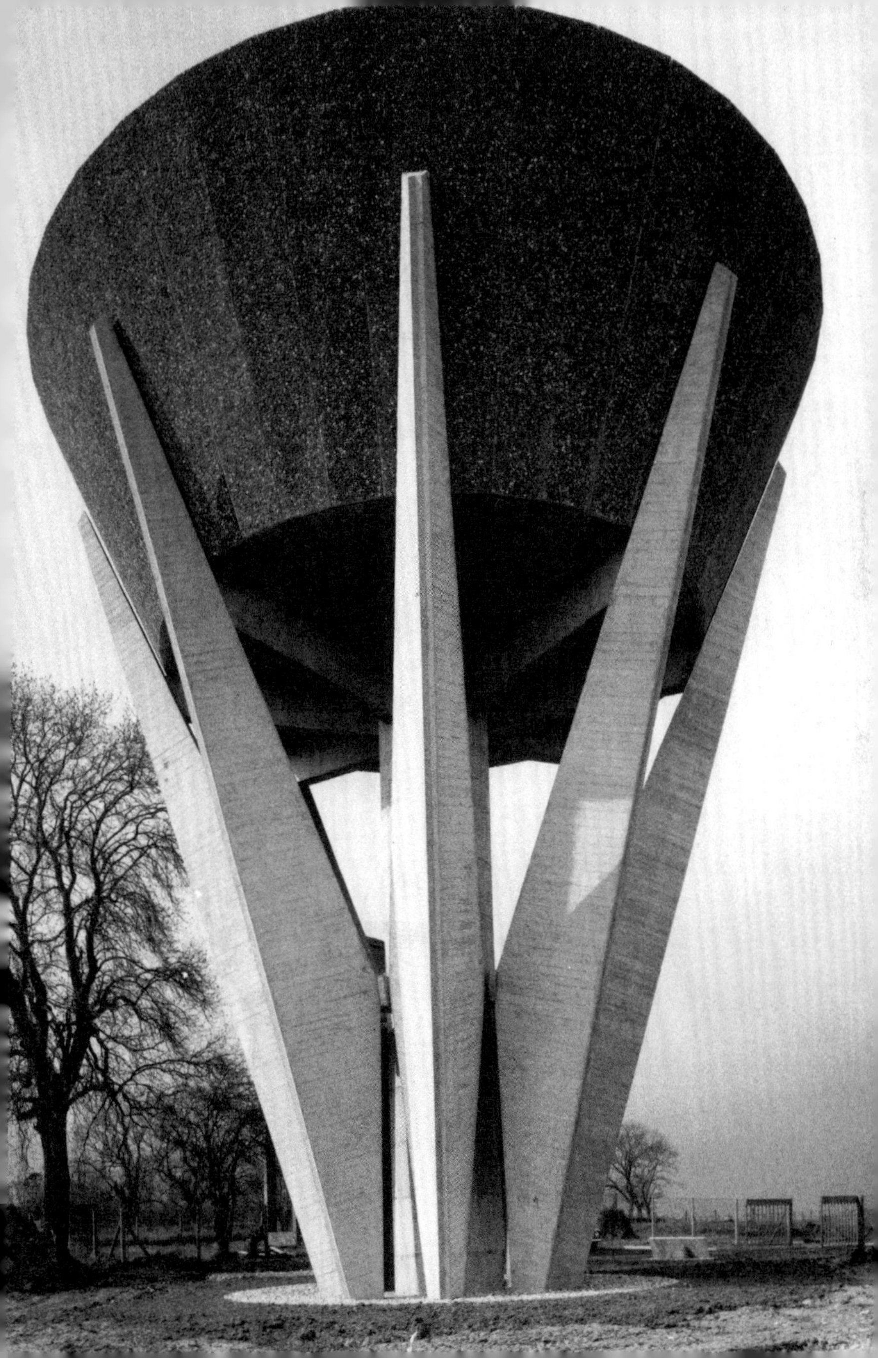

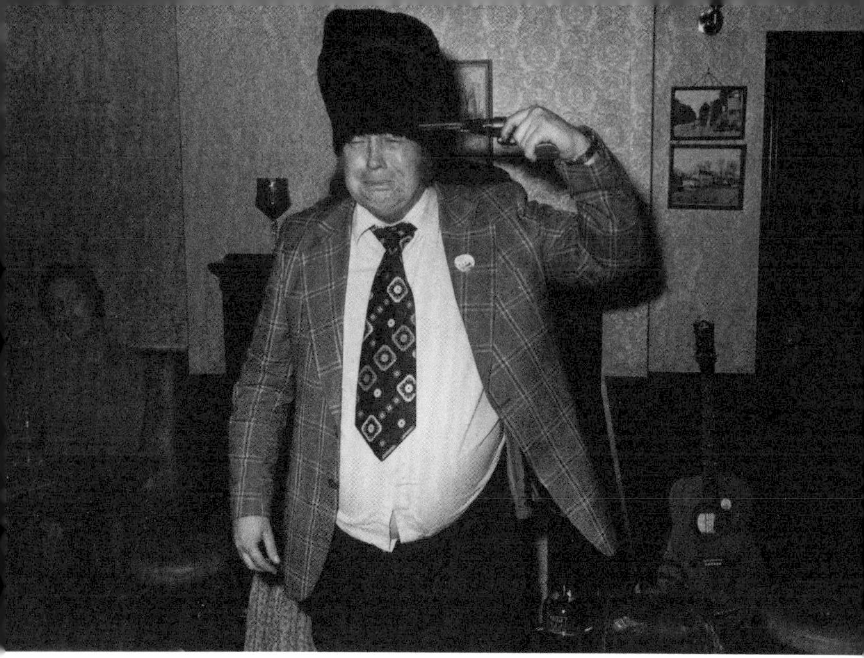

The suicide rate is soaring.

Young people are enrolled into local militias at Luton library.

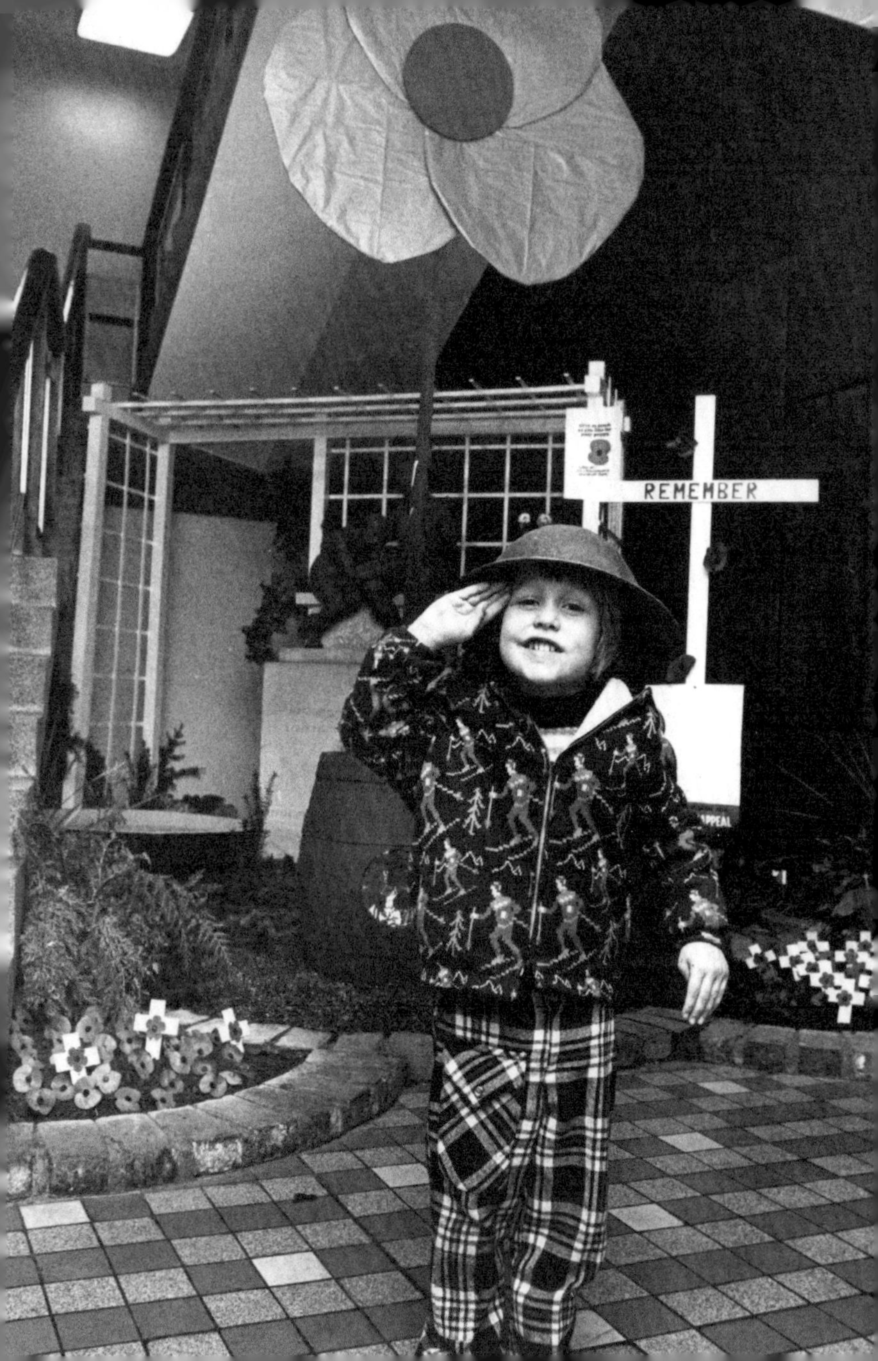
REMEMBER
APPEAL

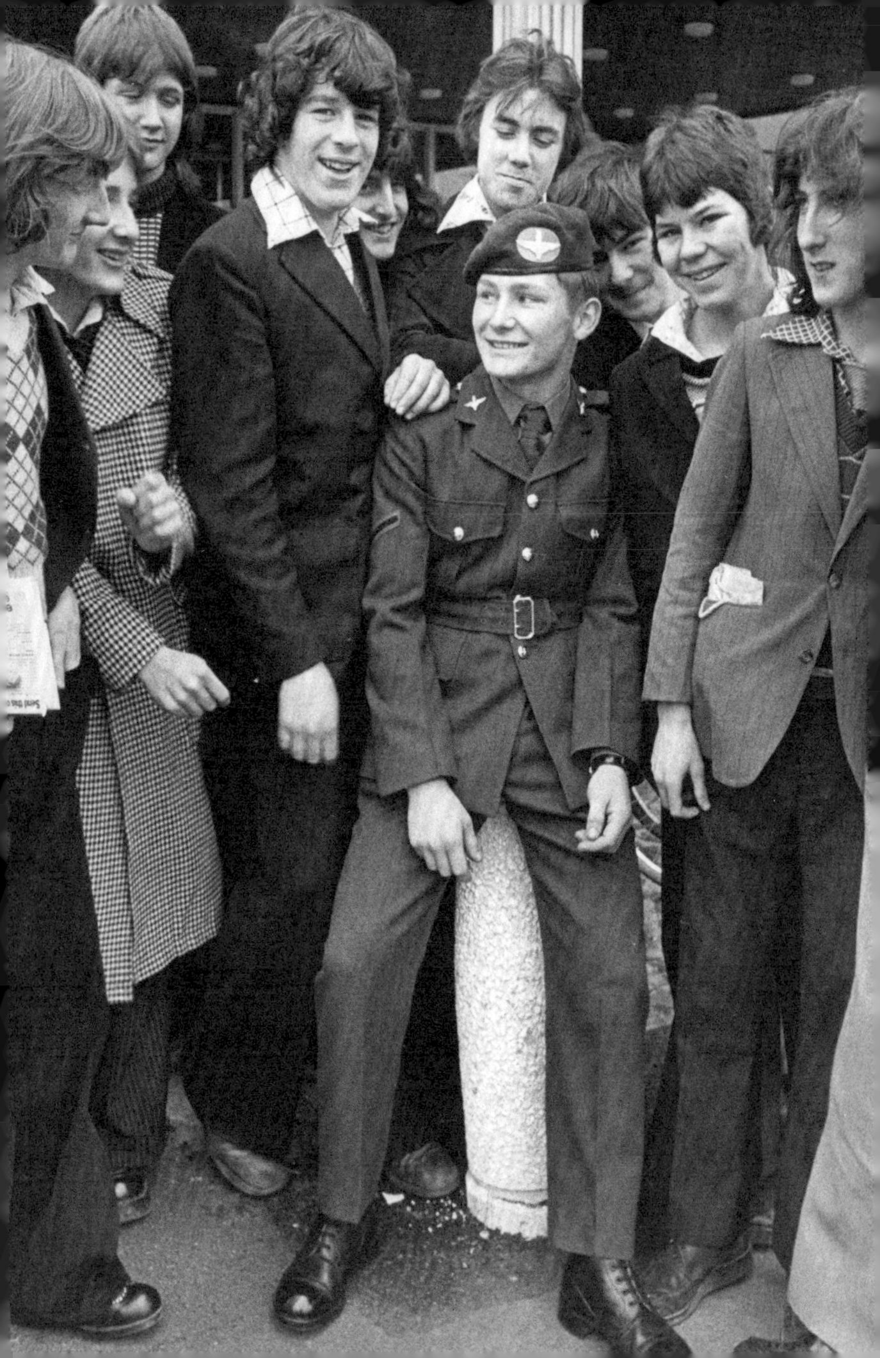

New recruits for the parachute regiment are signed up every day.

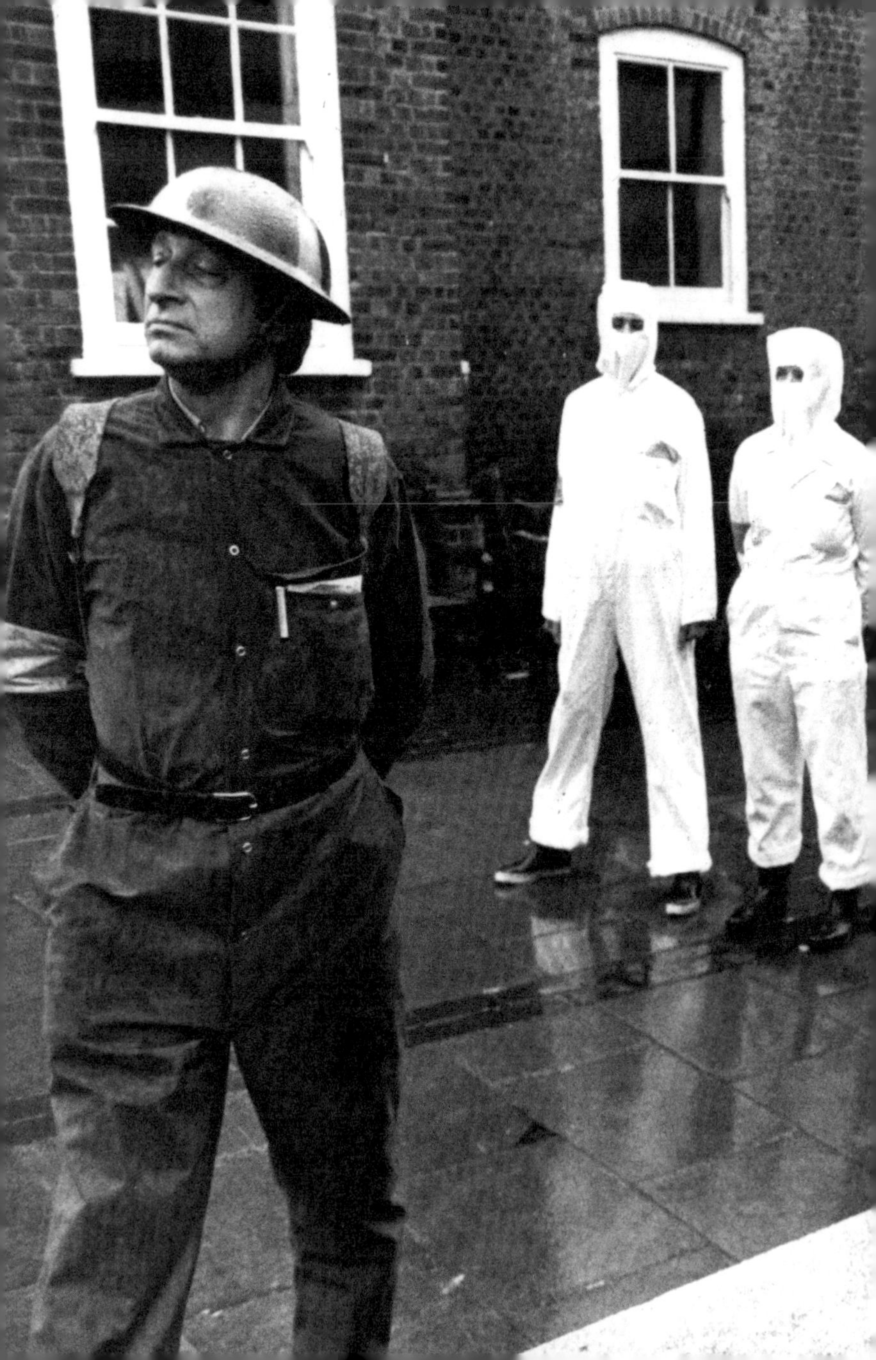

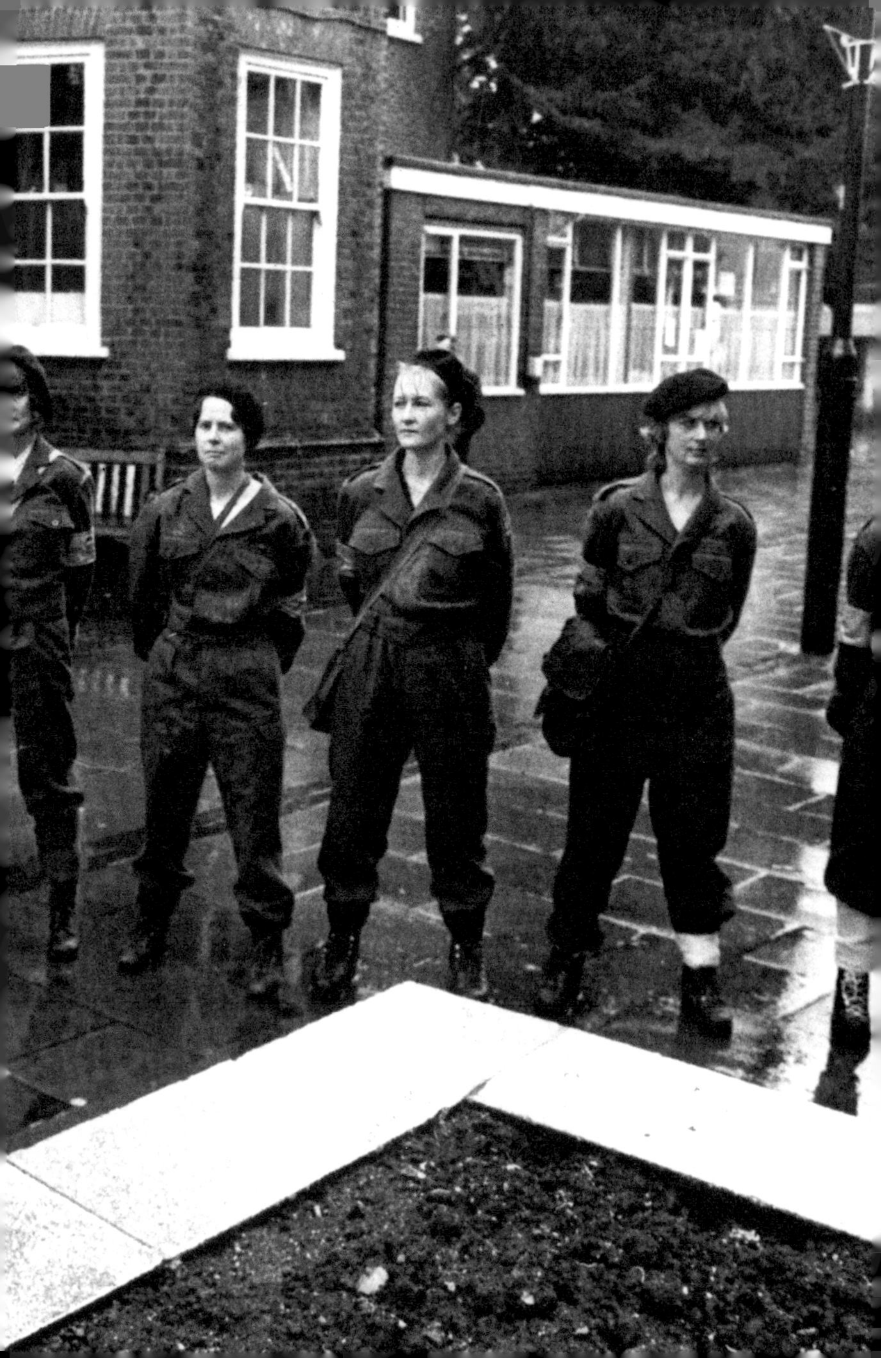

Civil defence corps are active
in each neighbourhood.

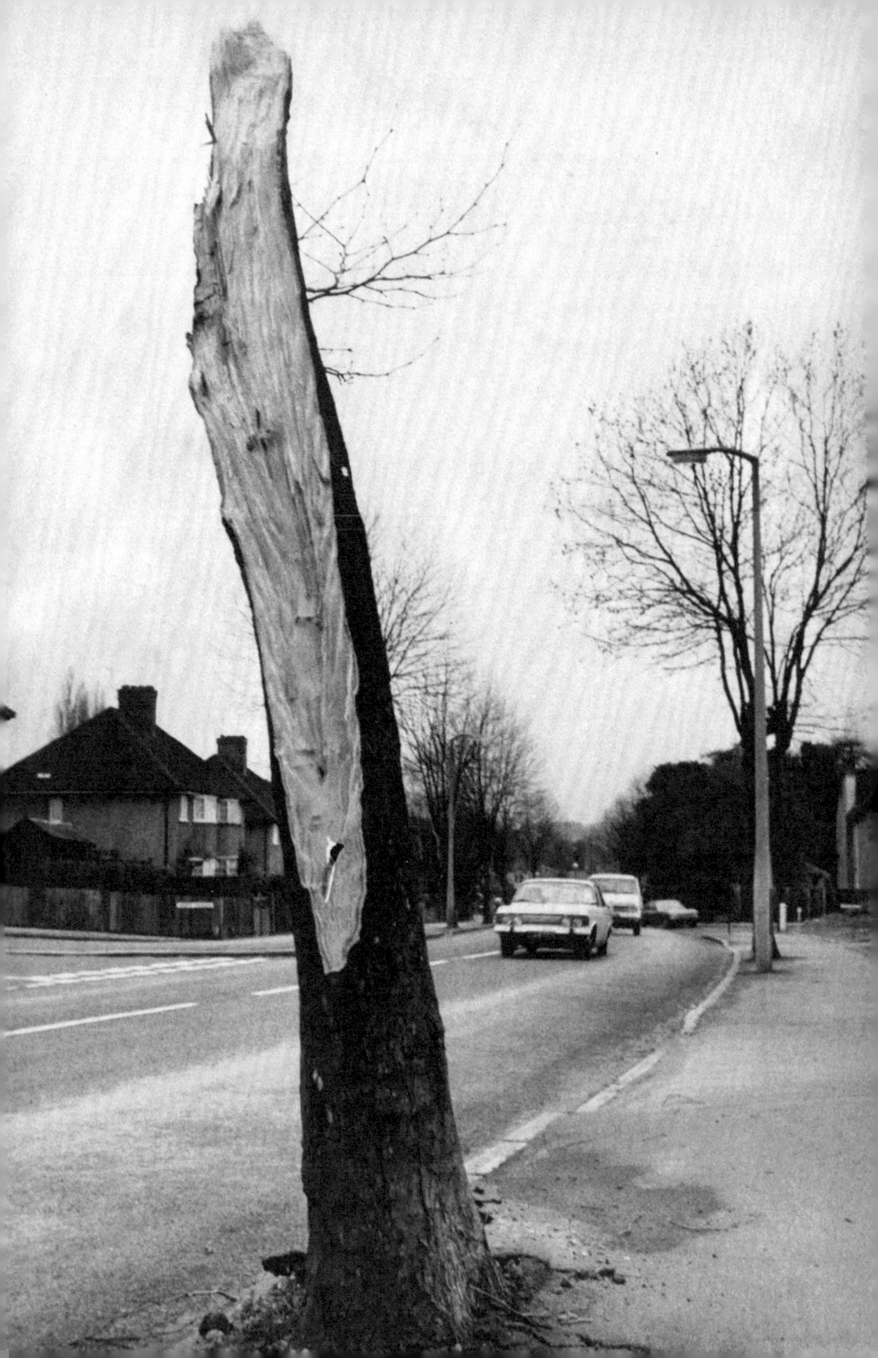

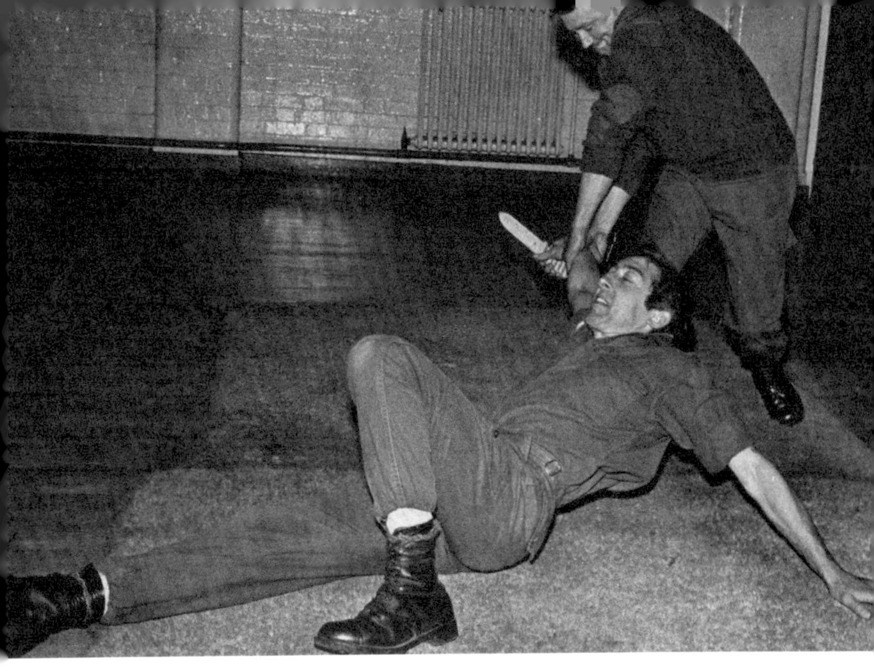

Army Shakespeare Companies are working alongside the community.

Man murdered by tree in Eastbury.

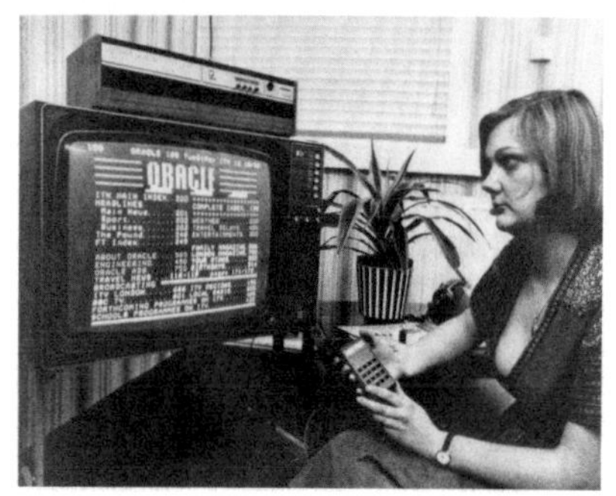

WRVS operate an Oracle Decoder System.

Young mystic shows where the rains came in.

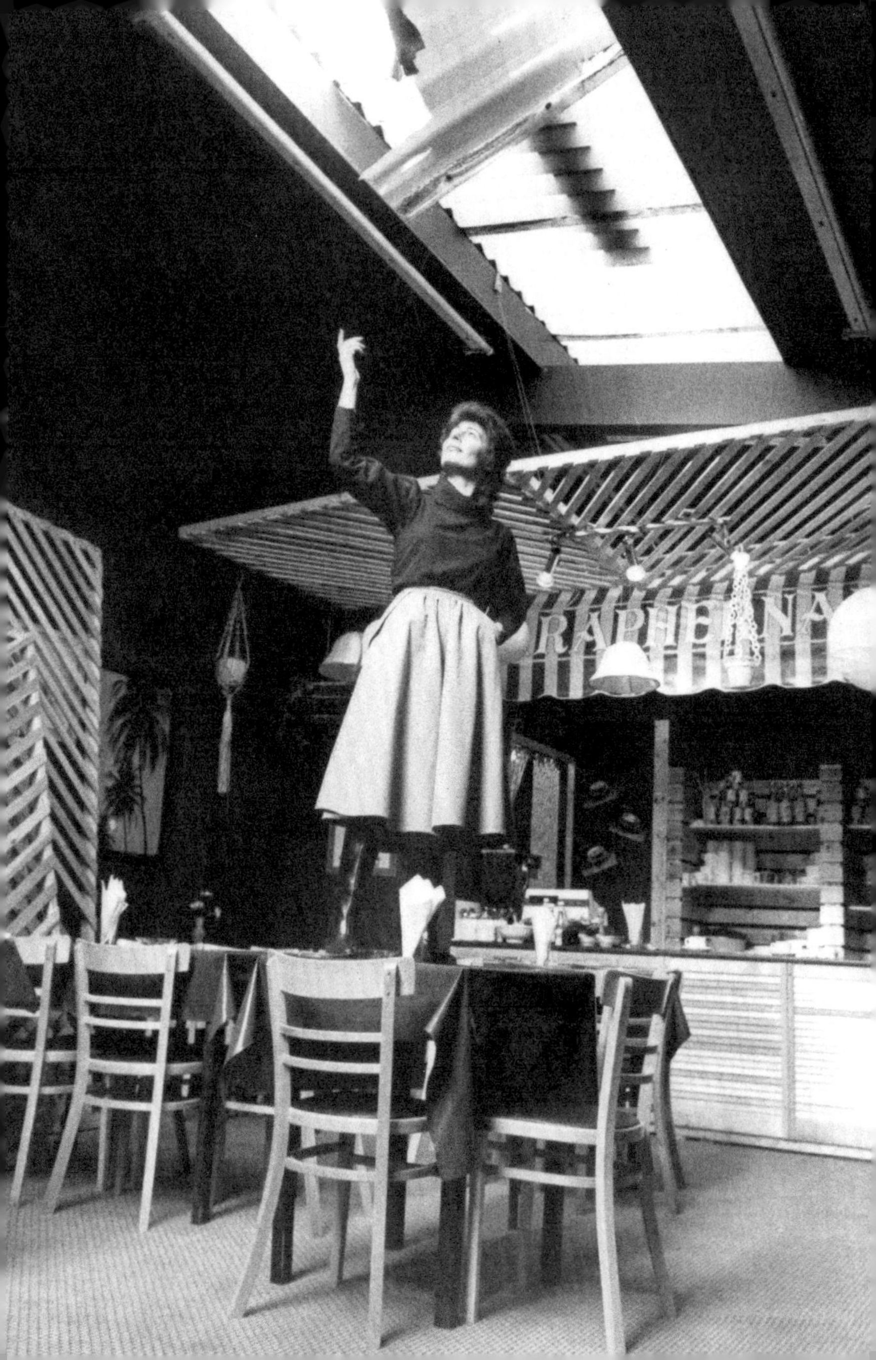

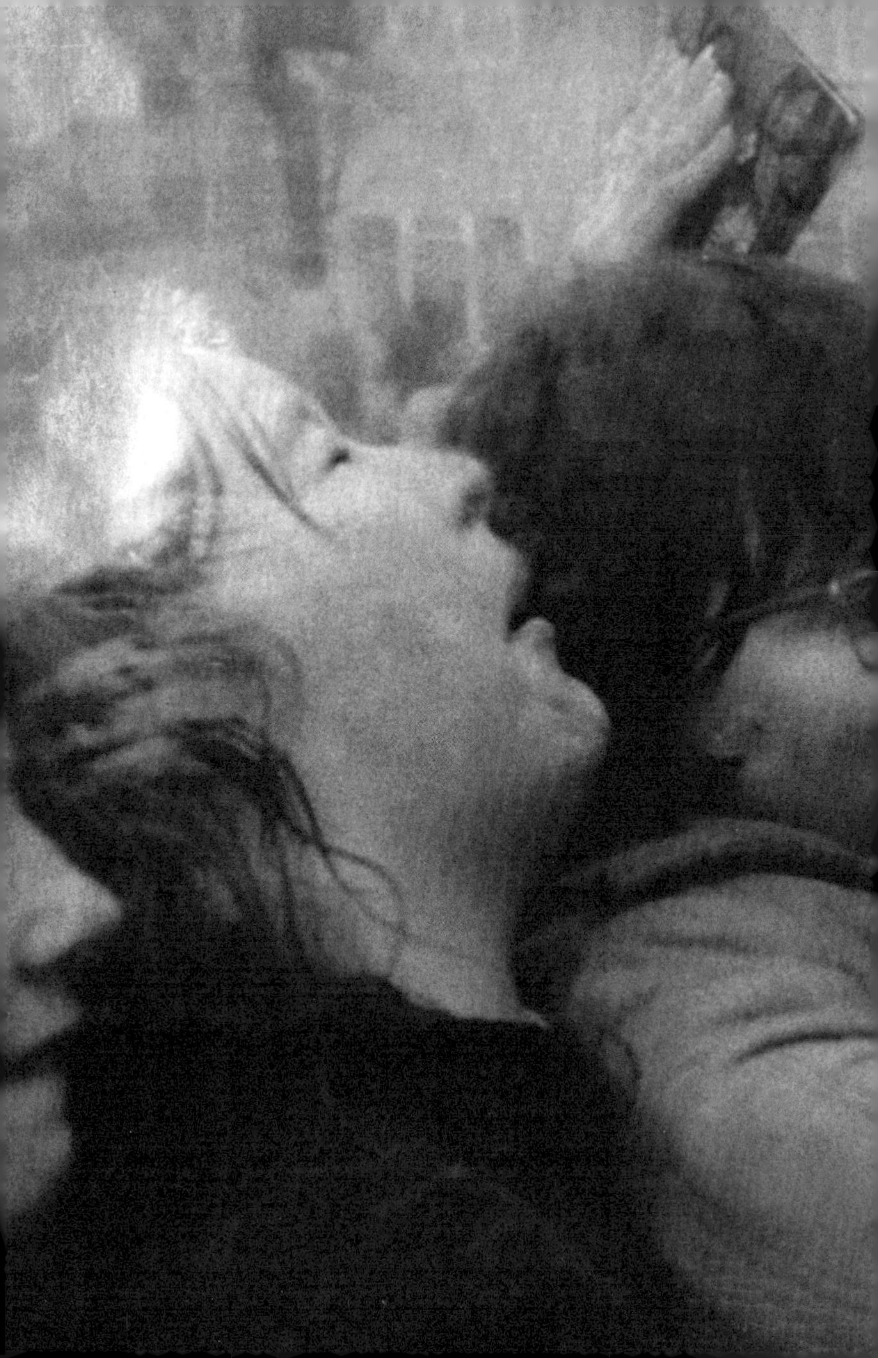

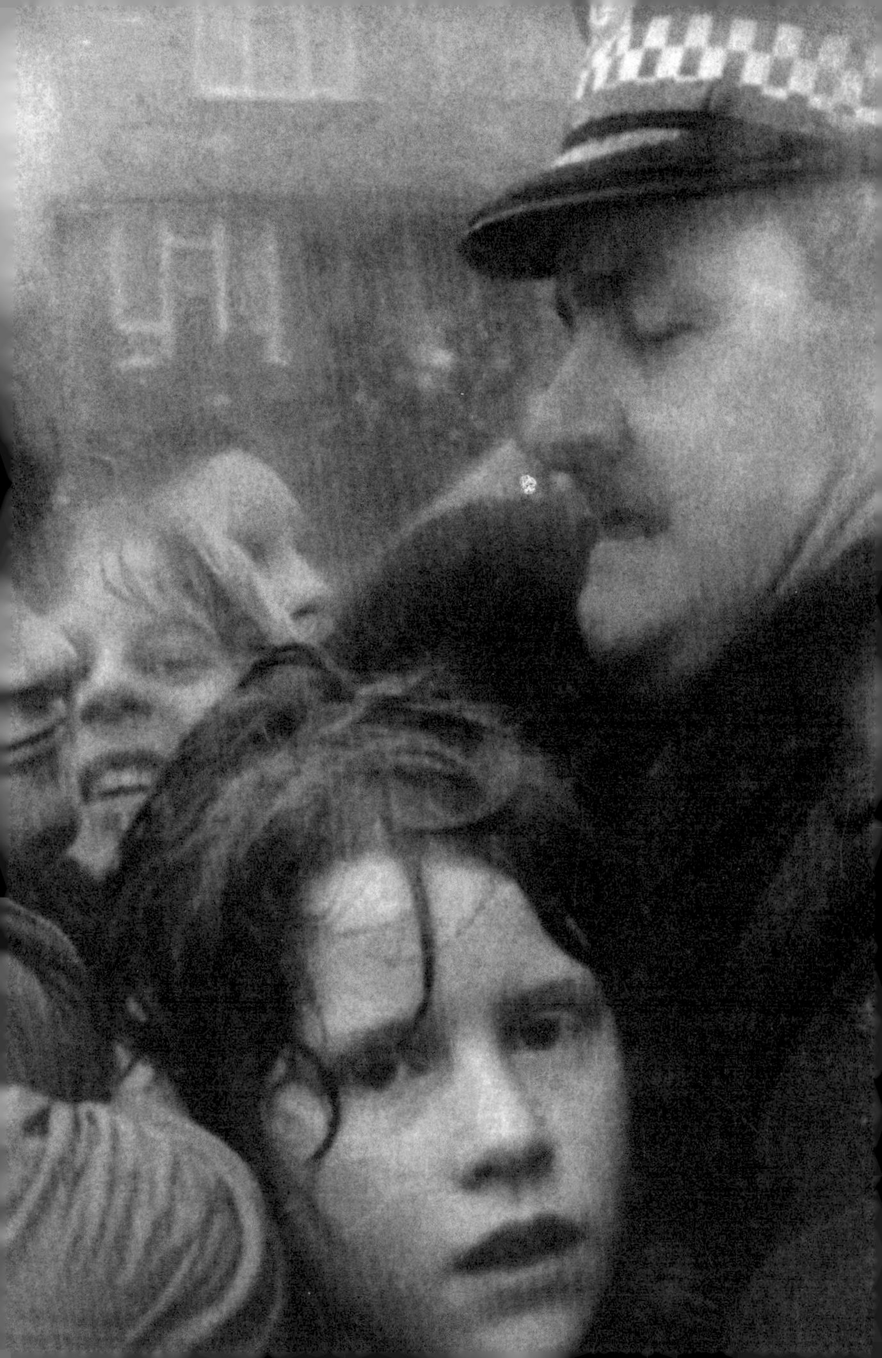

Mass hysteria is stretching police resources.

The Armed Forces and WRVS
are experimenting with robot
warriors.

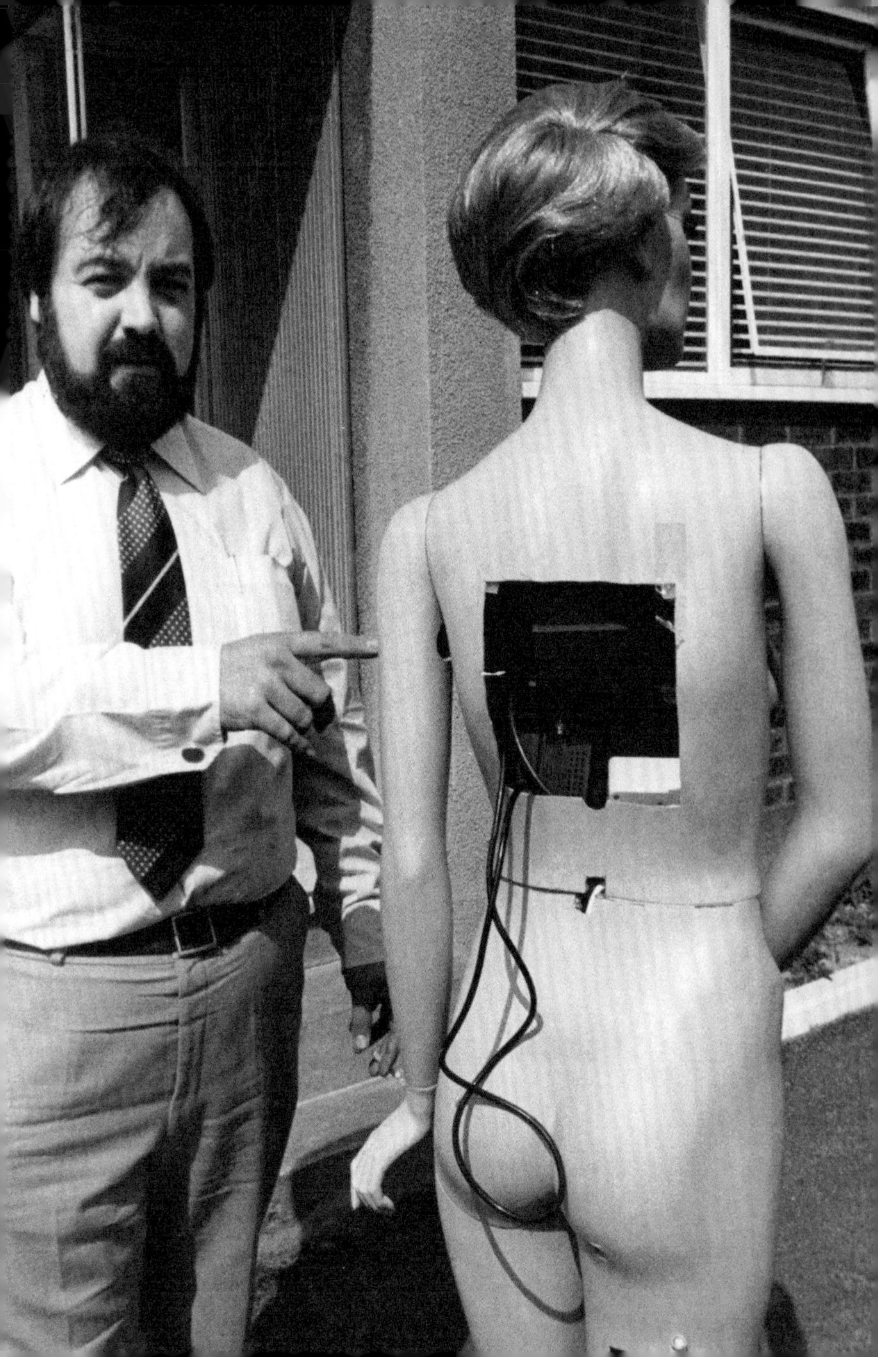

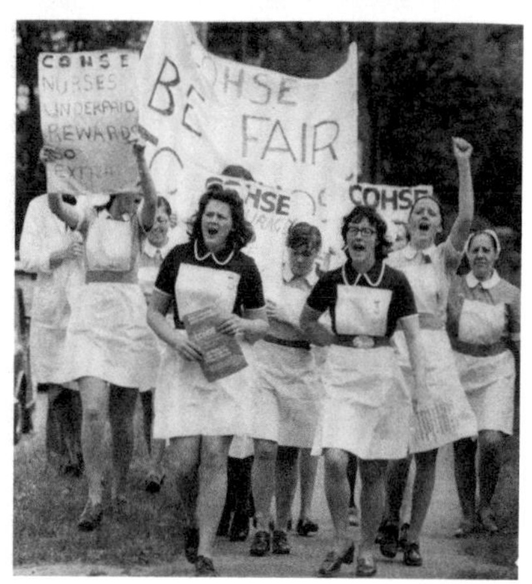

Nurses are in open rebellion.

All-girl units help in the fight for law and order.

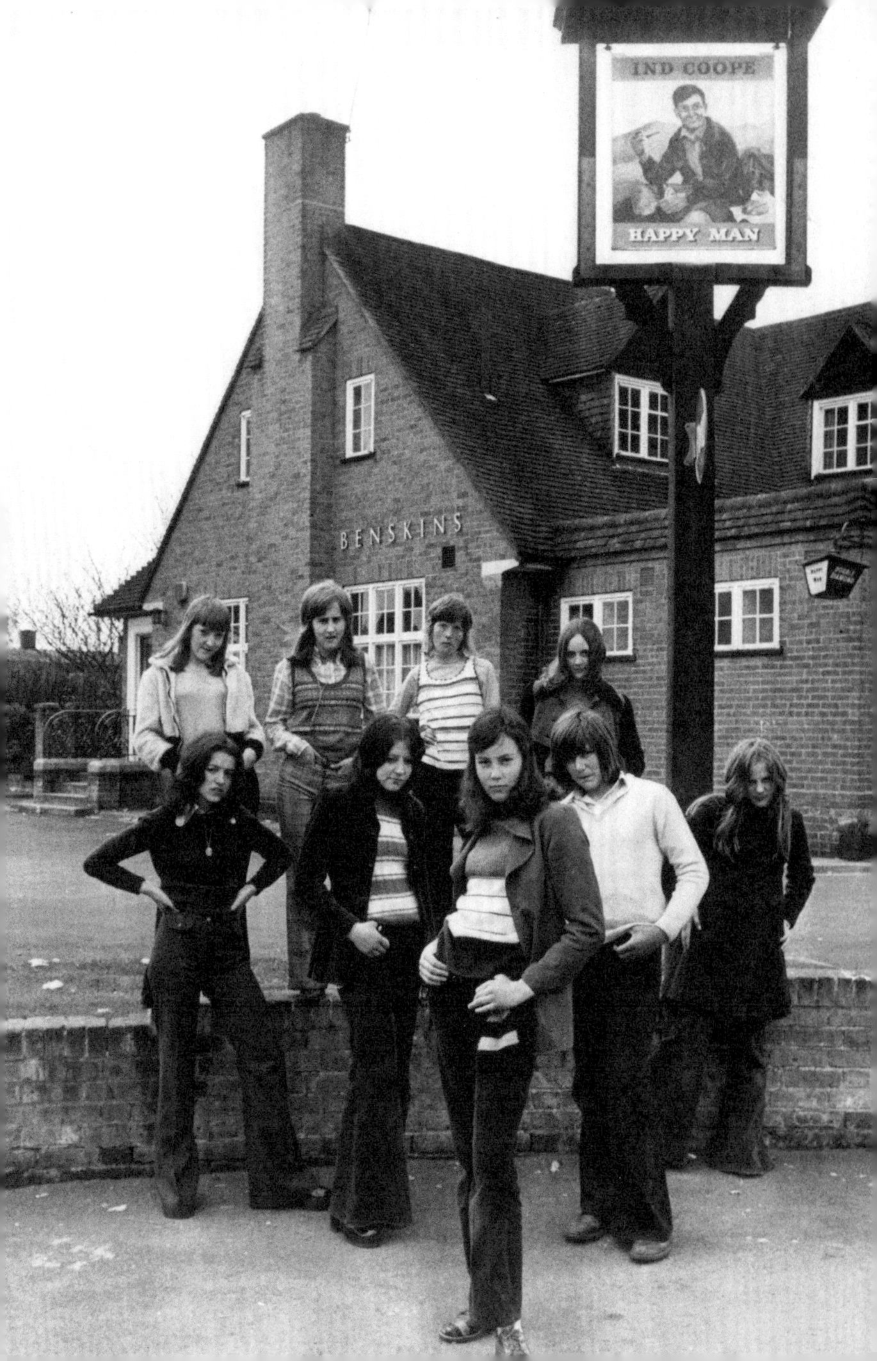
IND COOPE
HAPPY MAN
BENSKINS

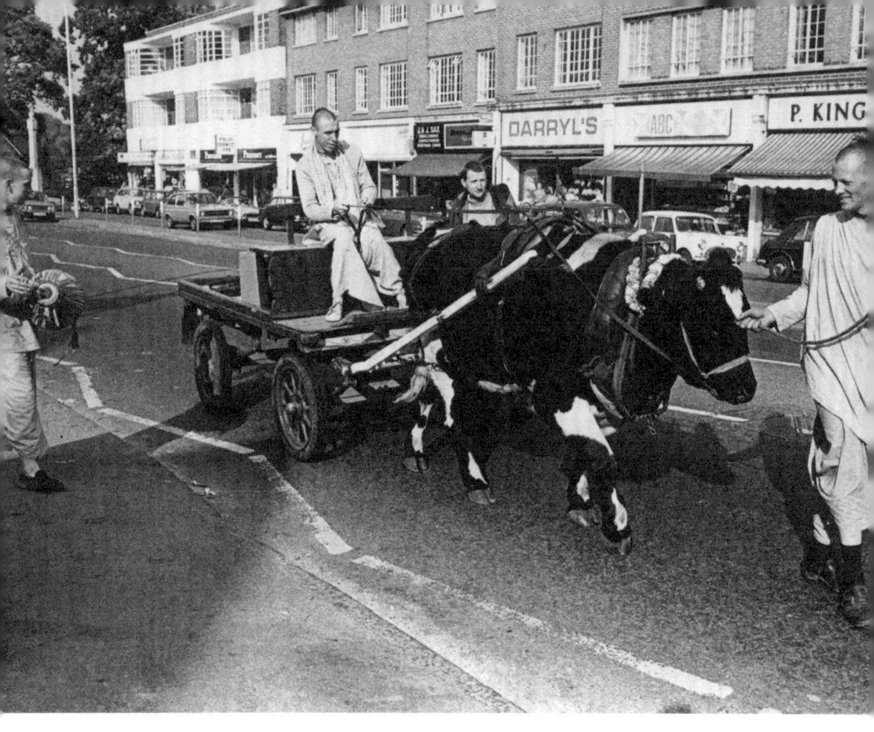

Cow worship is spreading through
the youth clubs.

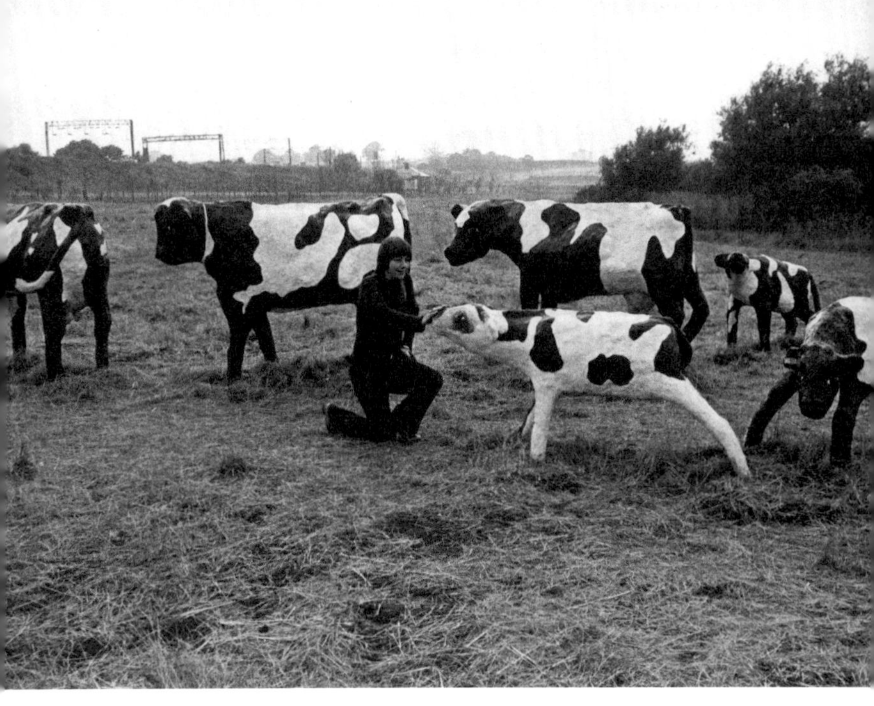

Idols appear in Milton Keynes.

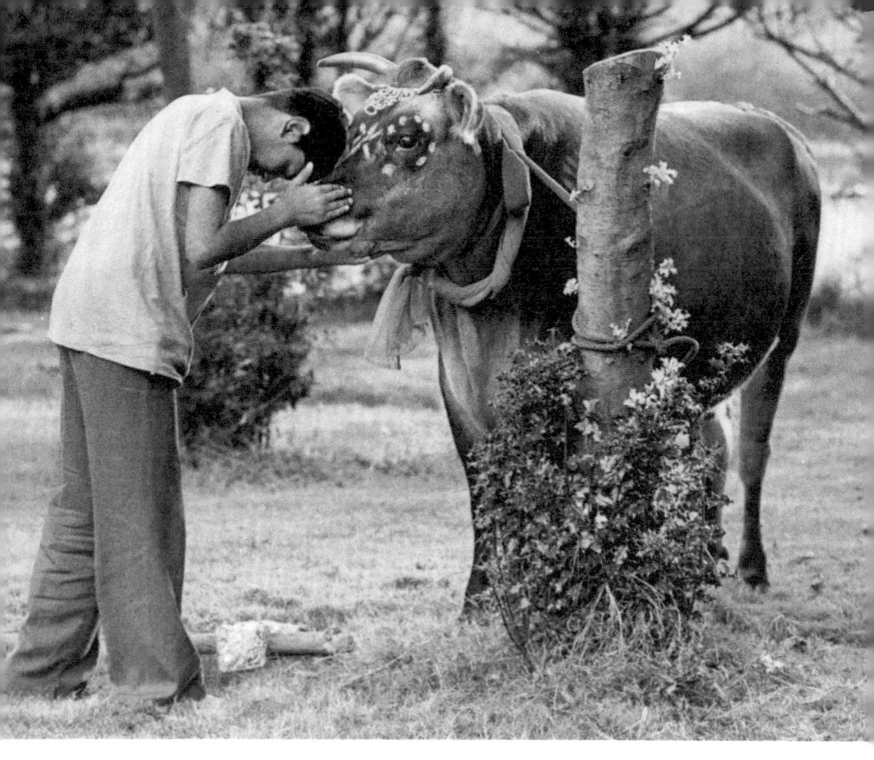

Watford youth worships cow.

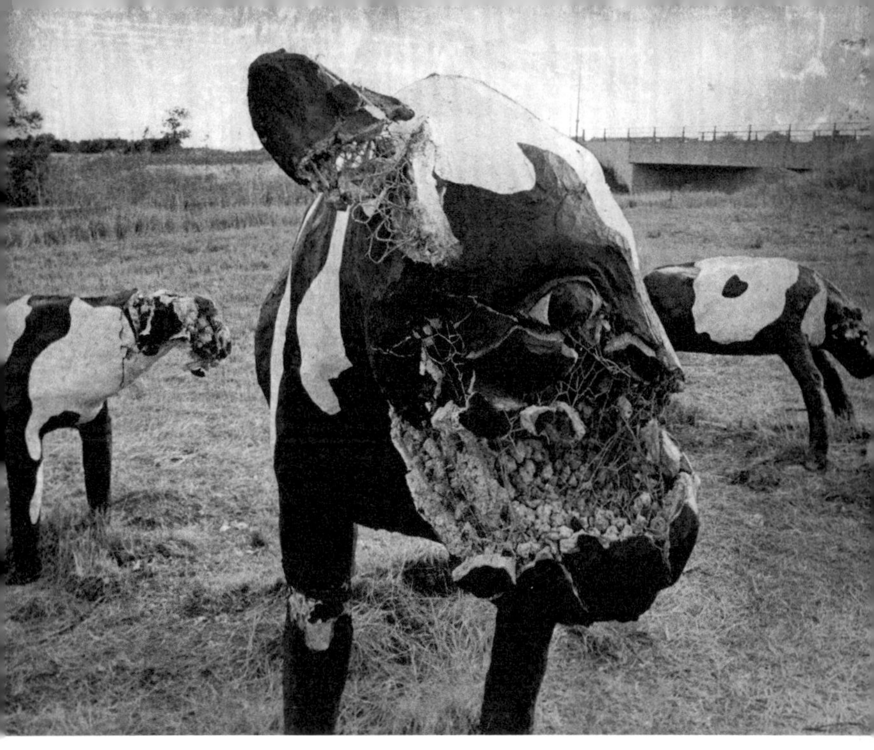

Cow idol disintegrates.

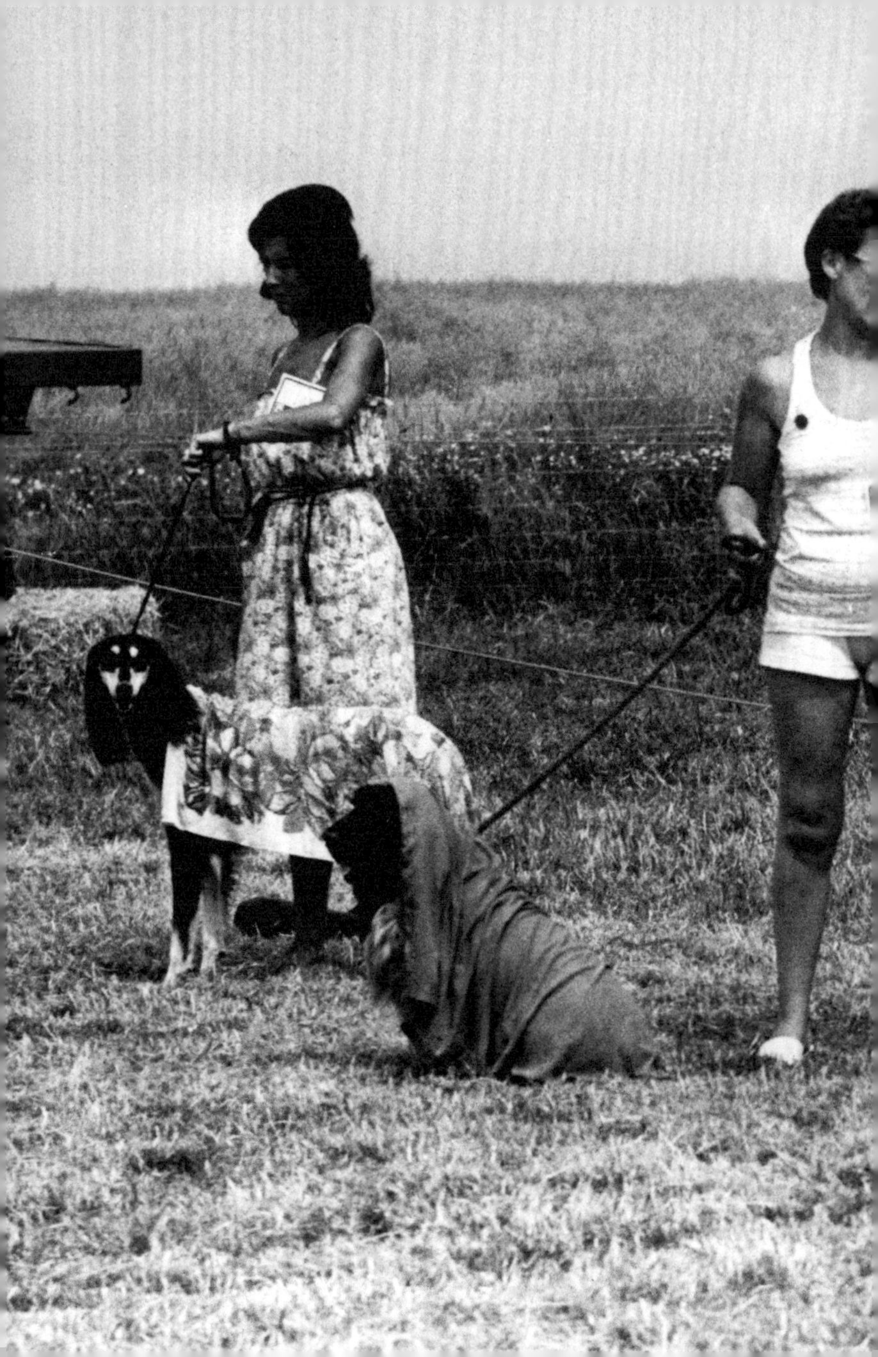

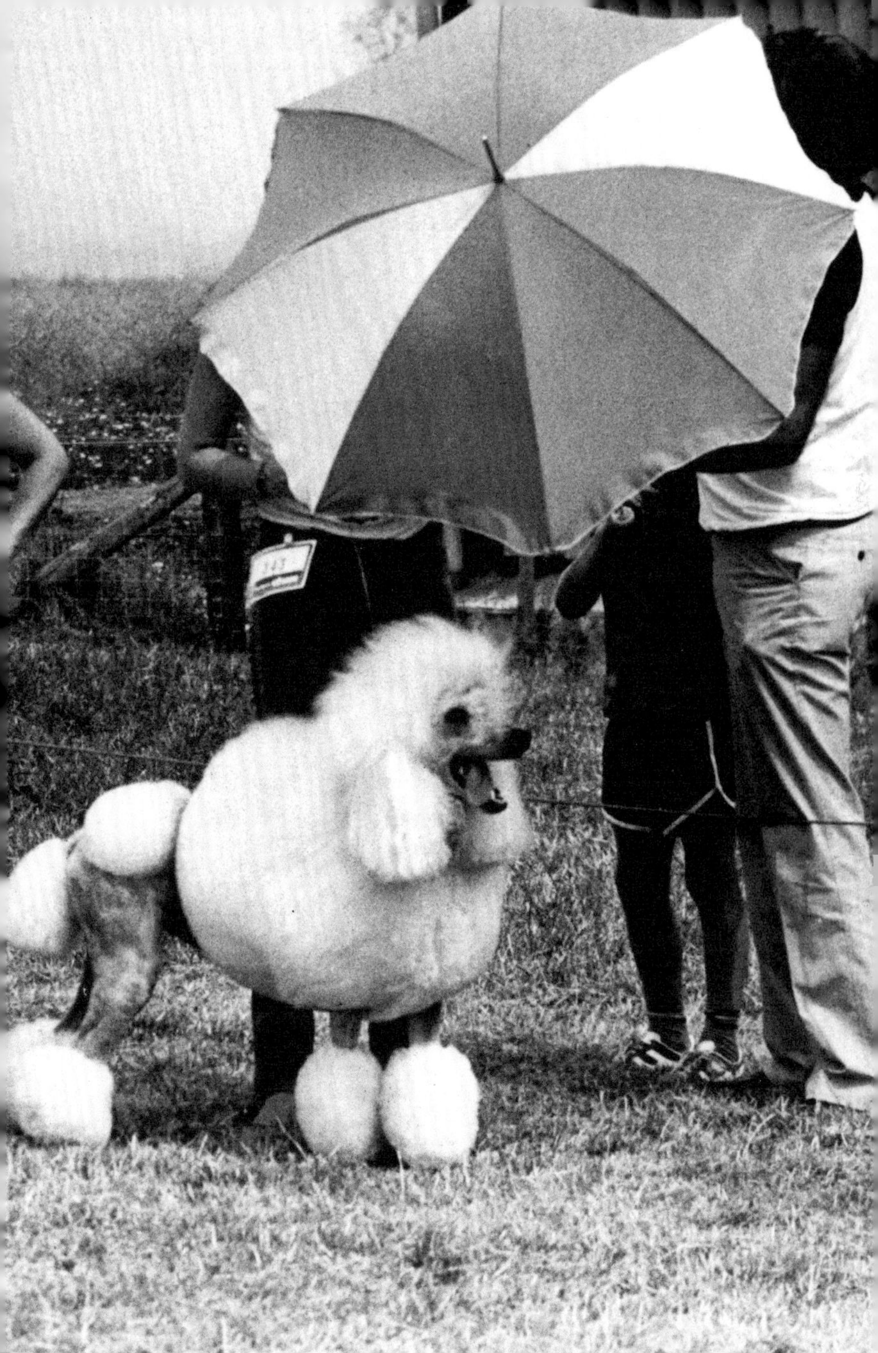

From a parasol a dog idol appears.

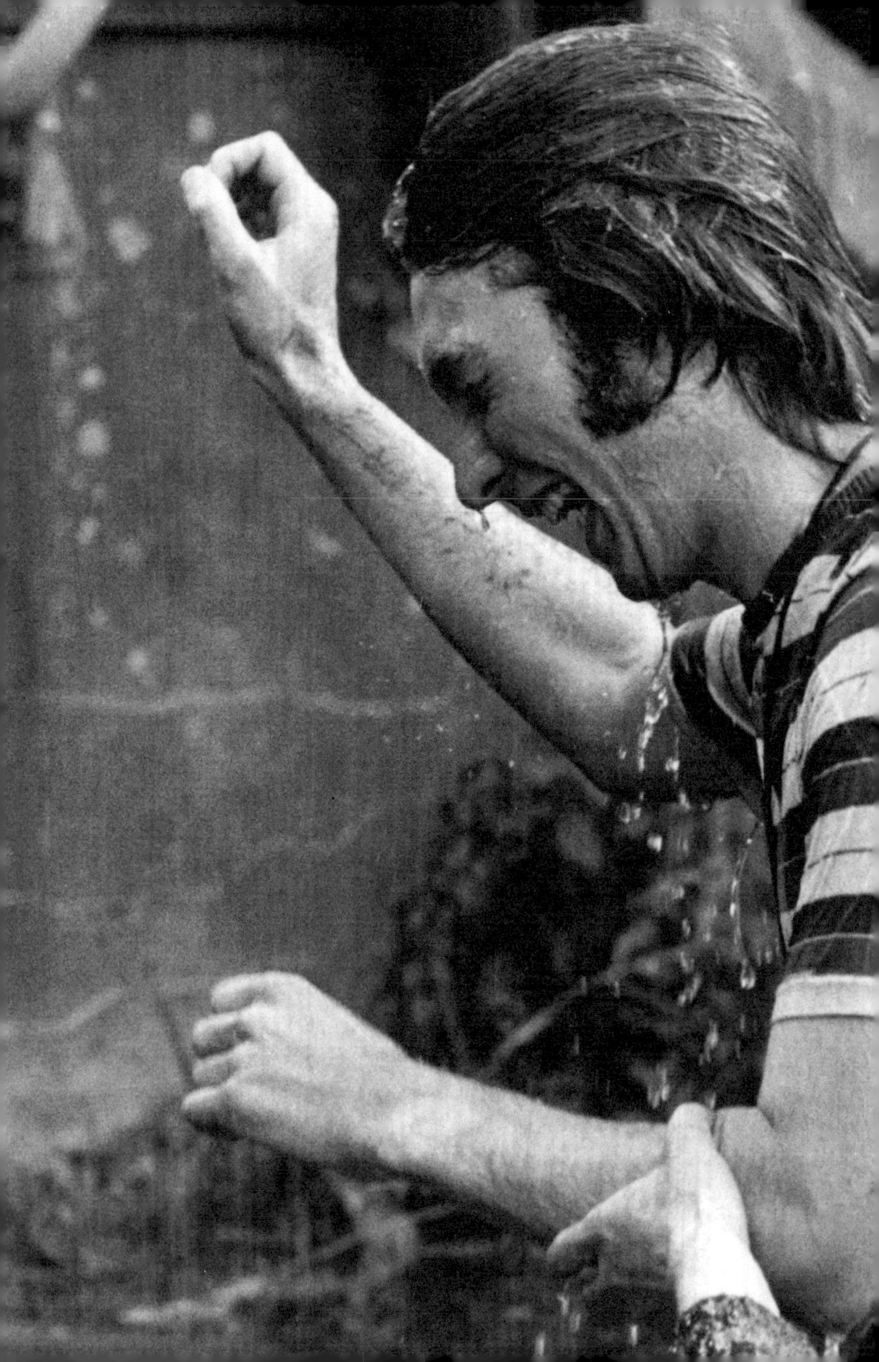

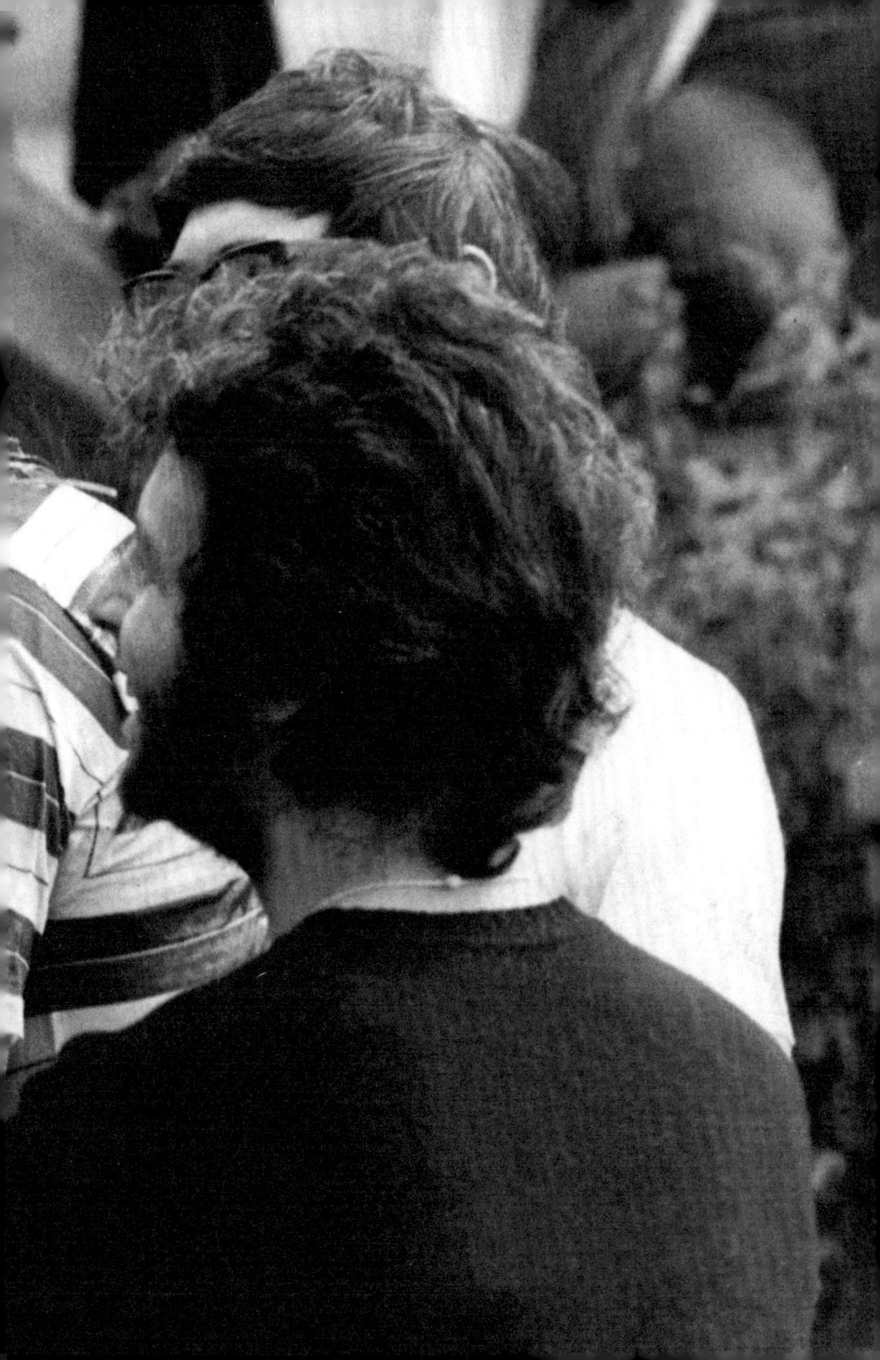

Steve Boxall and Geoff Elliot
baptising Bruce Saunders.

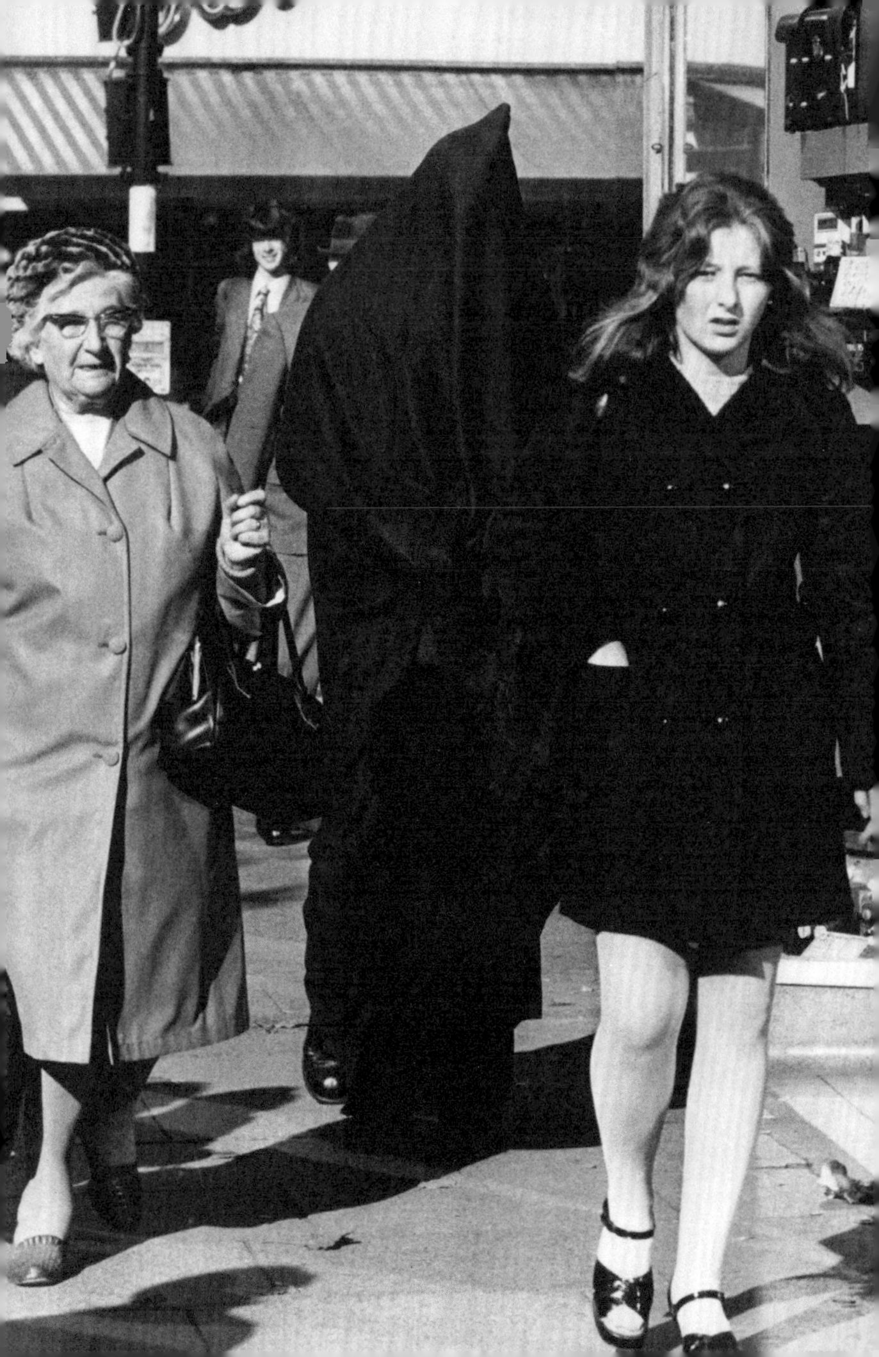

The Transmania Expedition,
Watford.

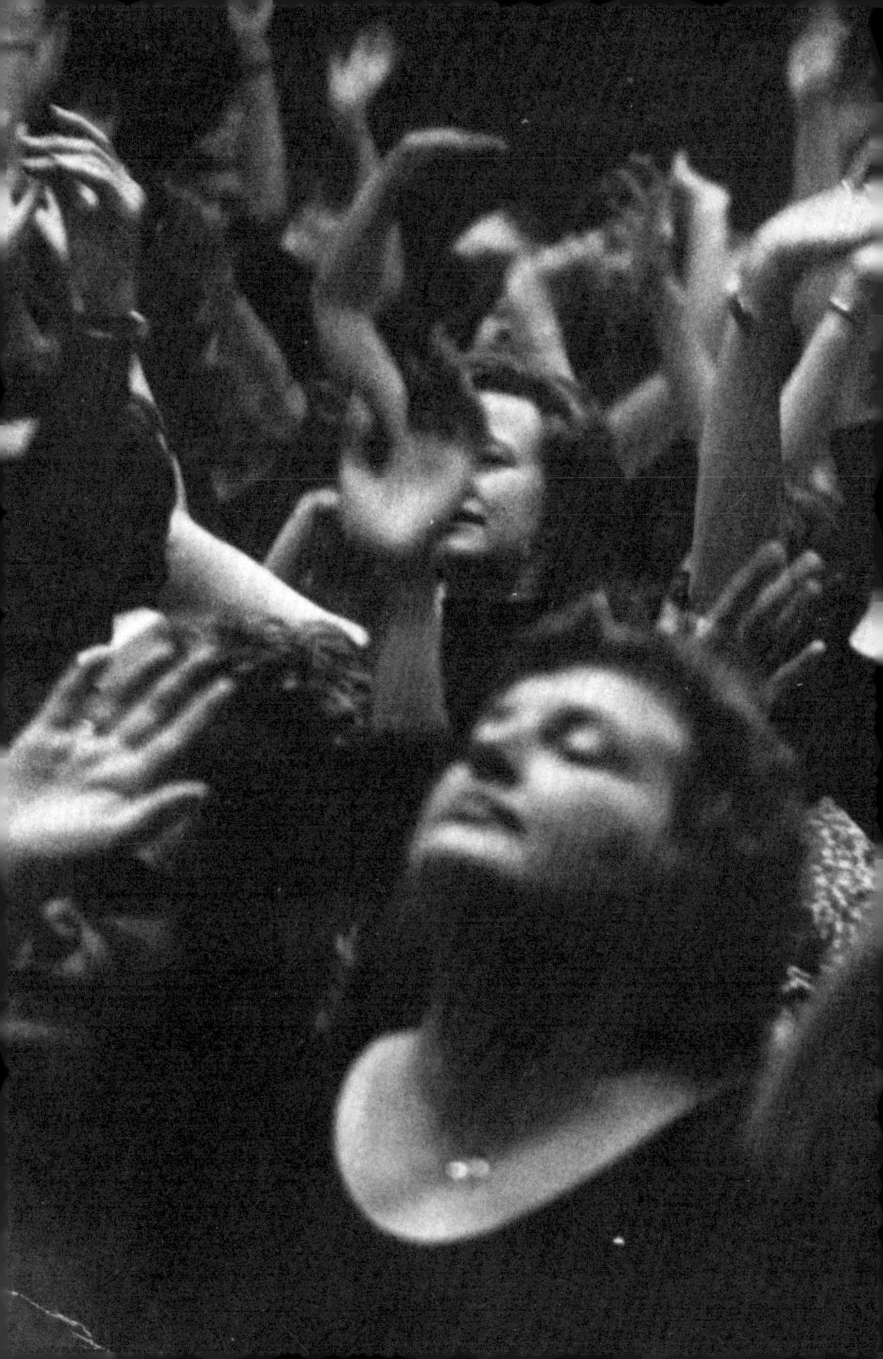

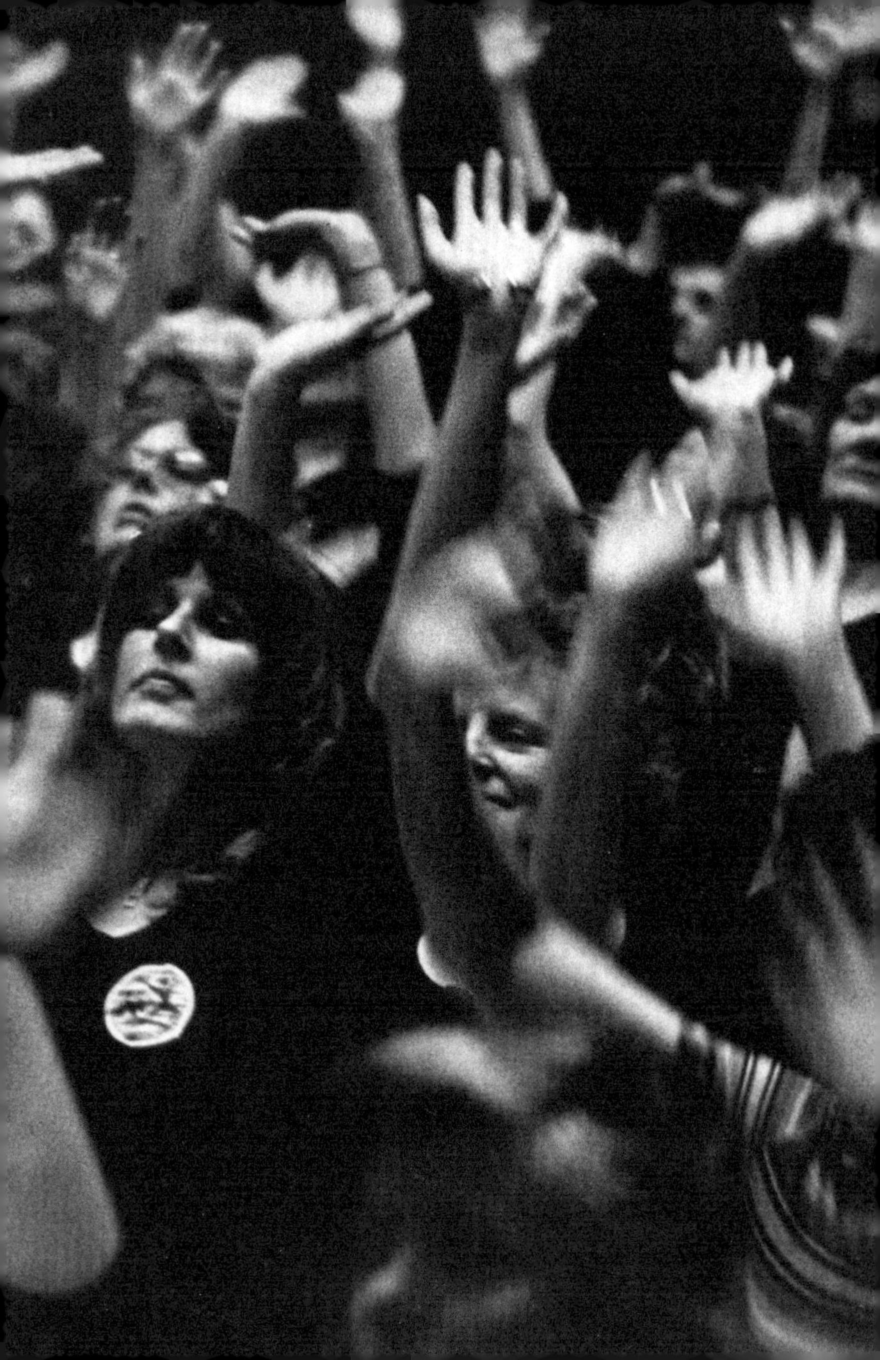

Deep in the heart of Watford Town Hall, girls and ladies rally for women.

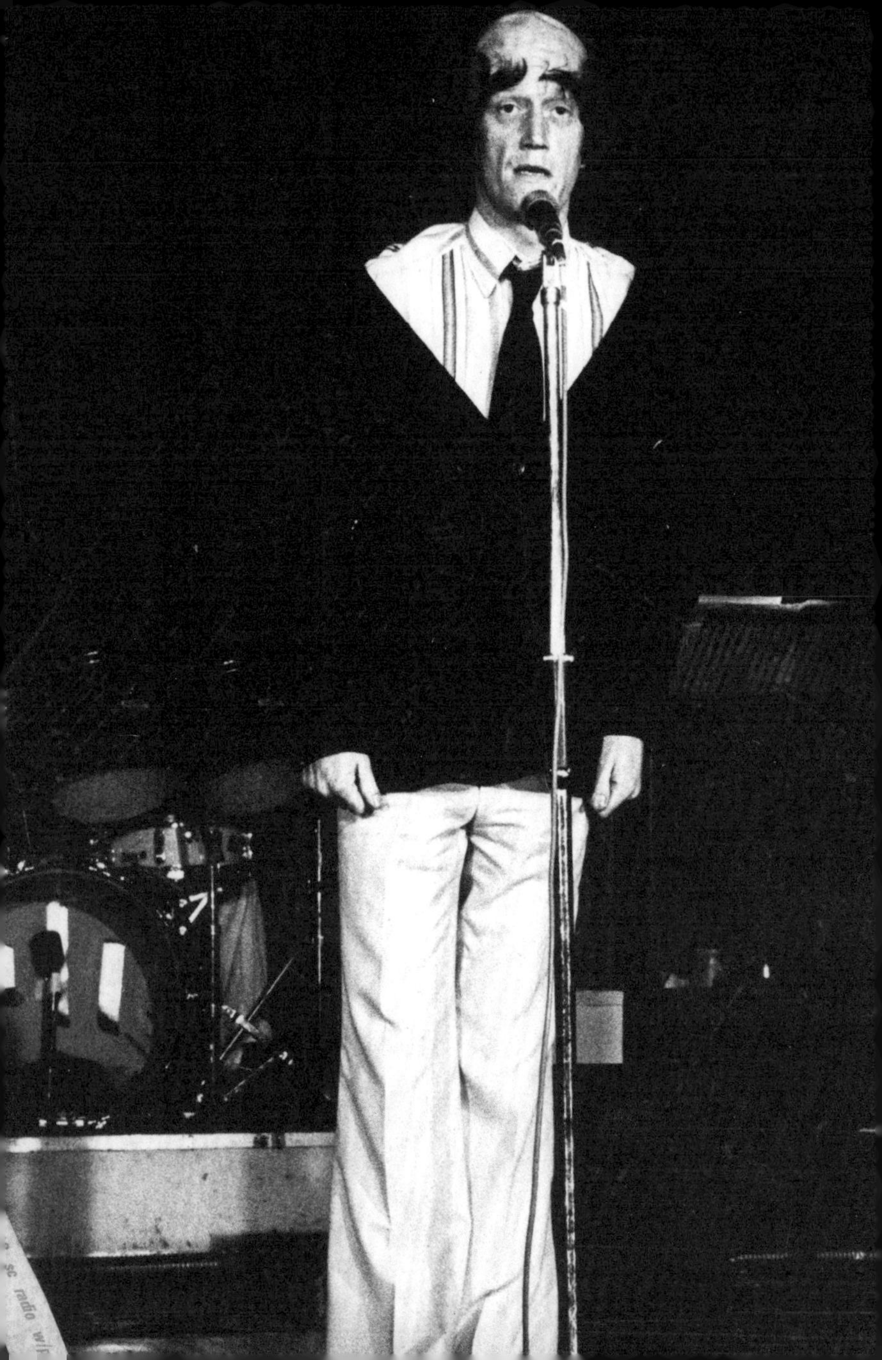

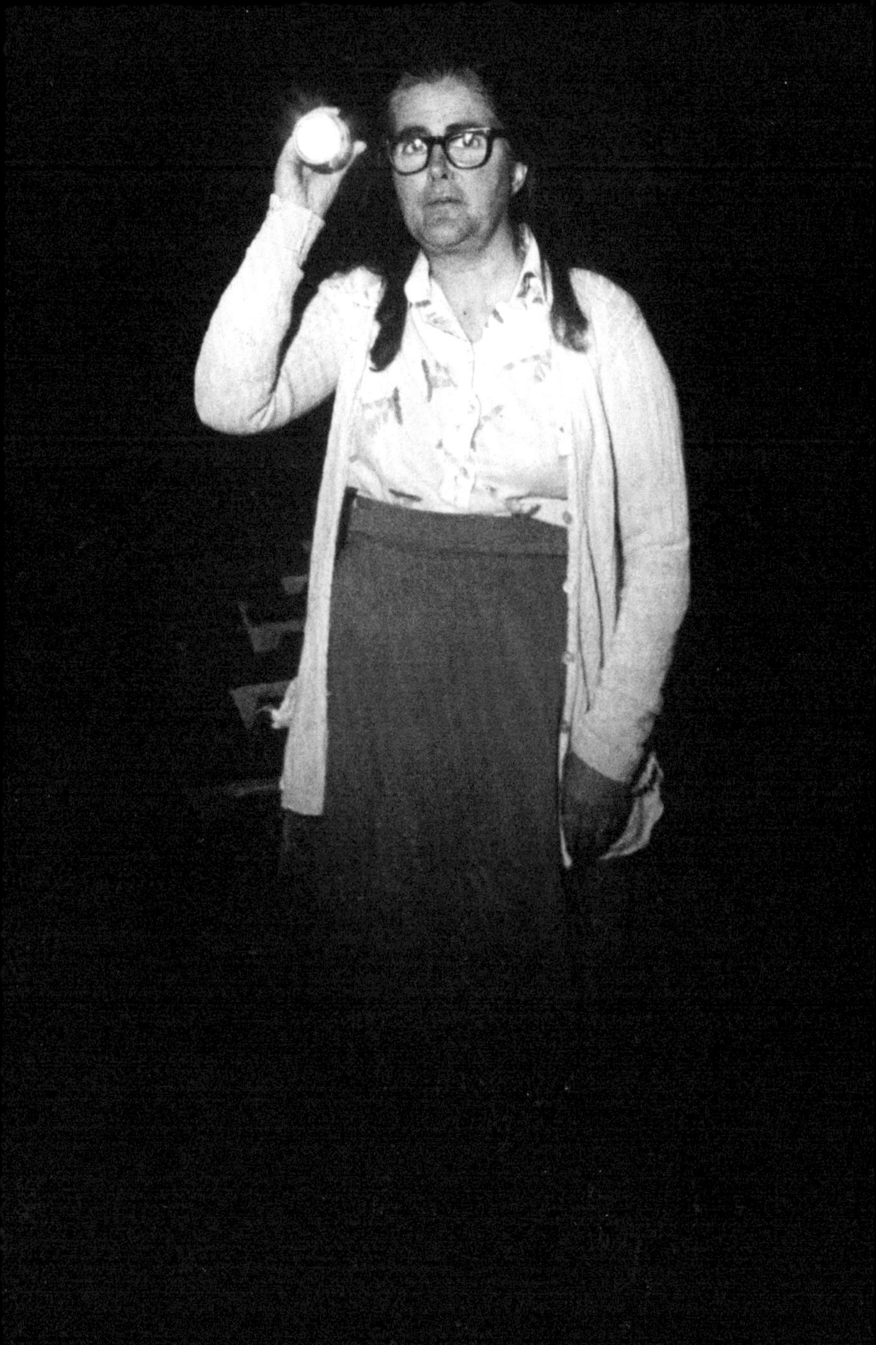

Evangelist predicts forthcoming events.

Usherette at a congregation in Borehamwood.

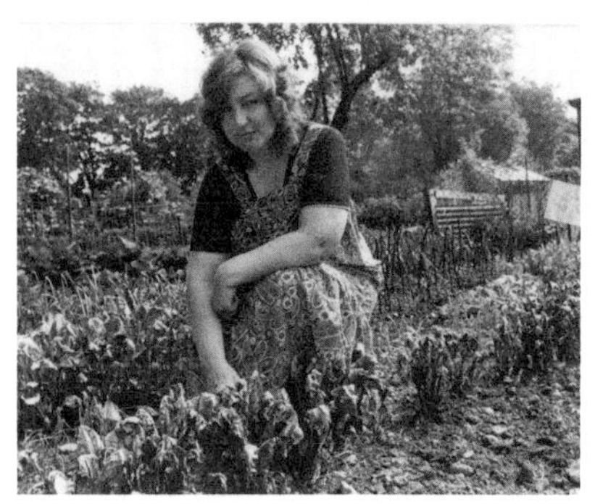

Abnormal plant damage, Holywell Hill.

Horticultural festival, Letchmore Heath.

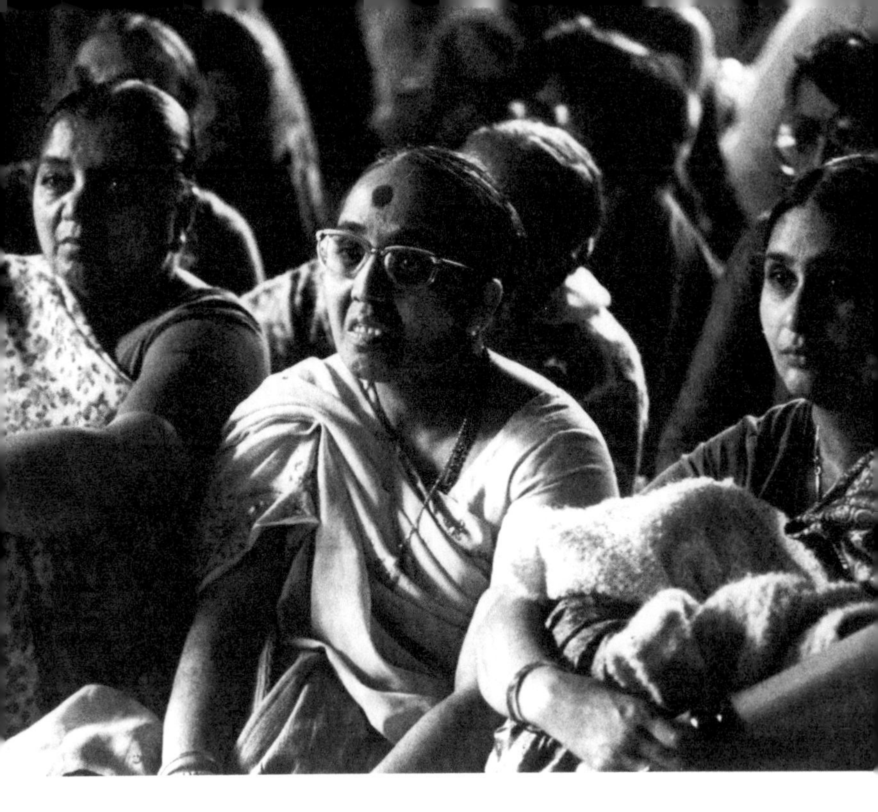

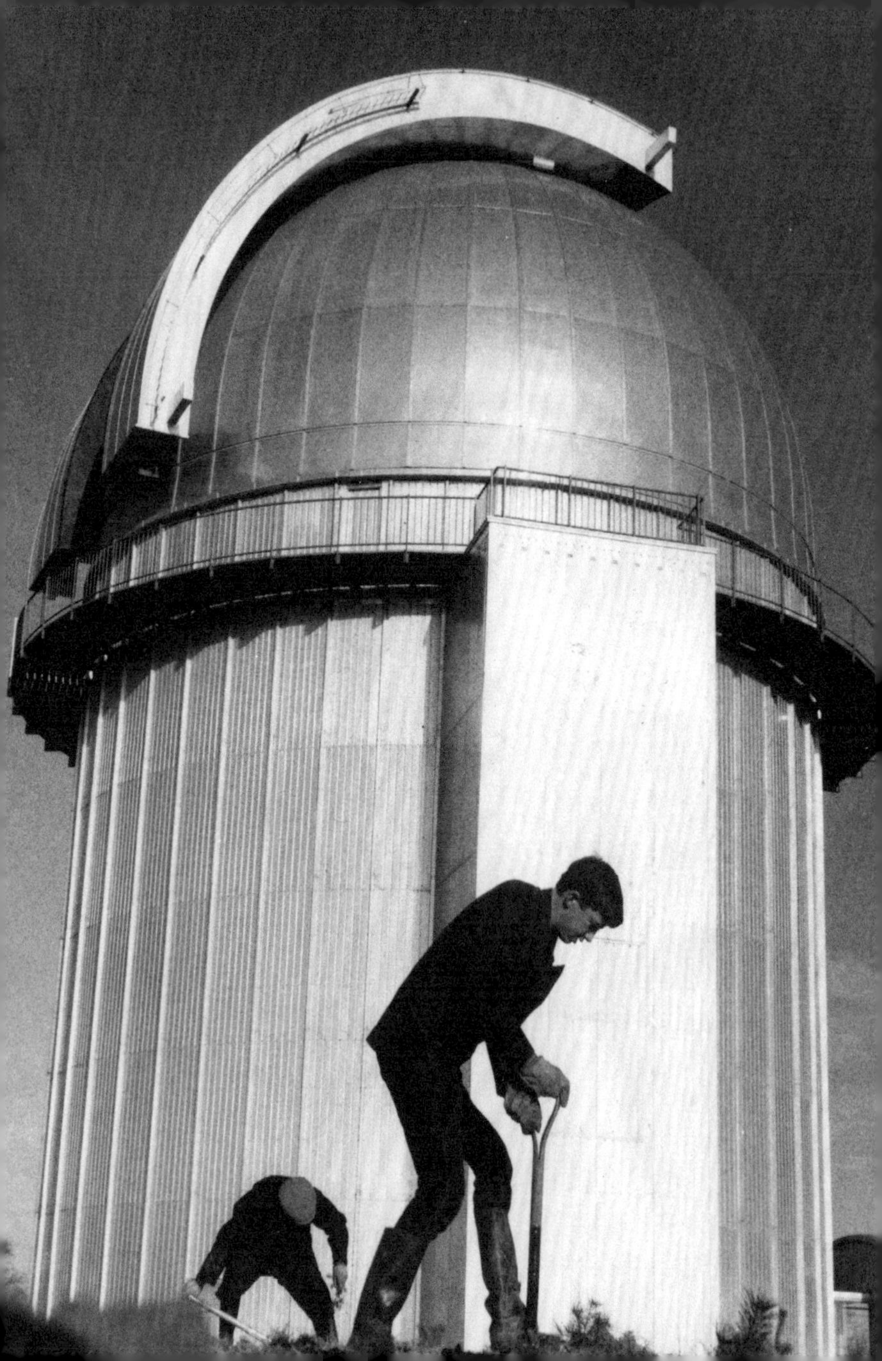

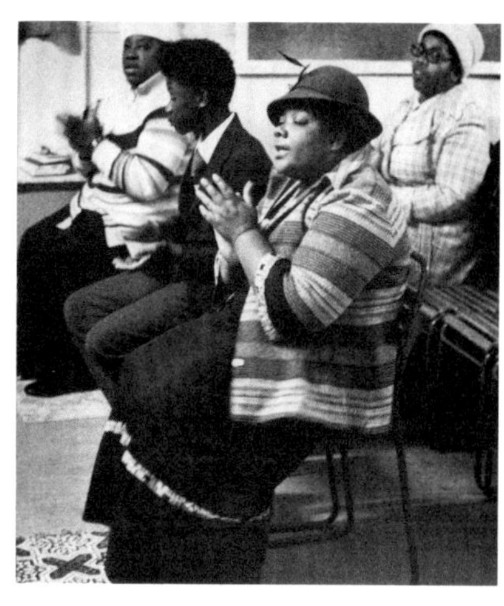

Israelite congregation.

The Queen will sit in the seat tomorrow and study the stars. Meanwhile the gardeners search the earth for clues.

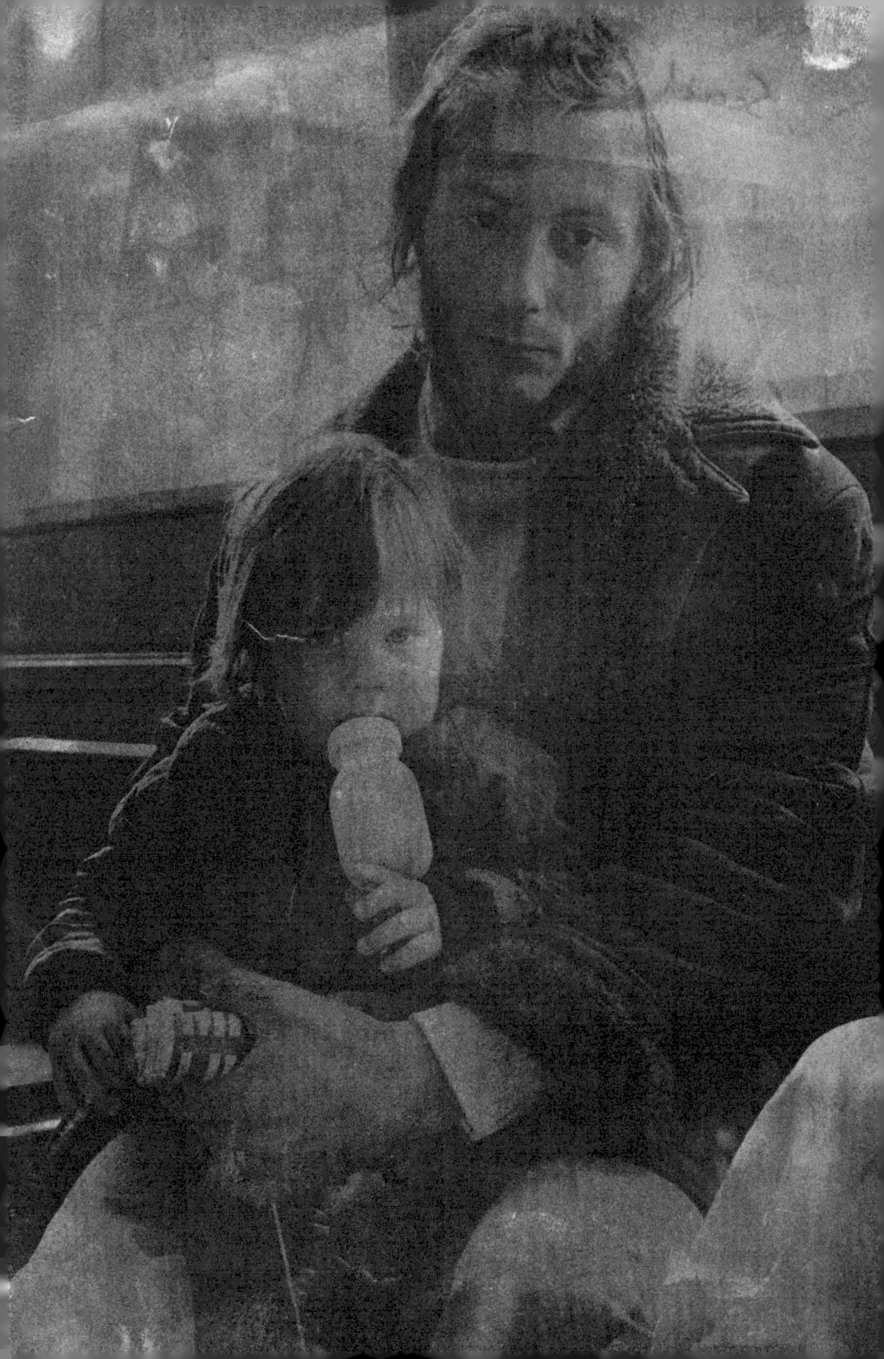

The social security office at Bletchley will not give any money for rent.

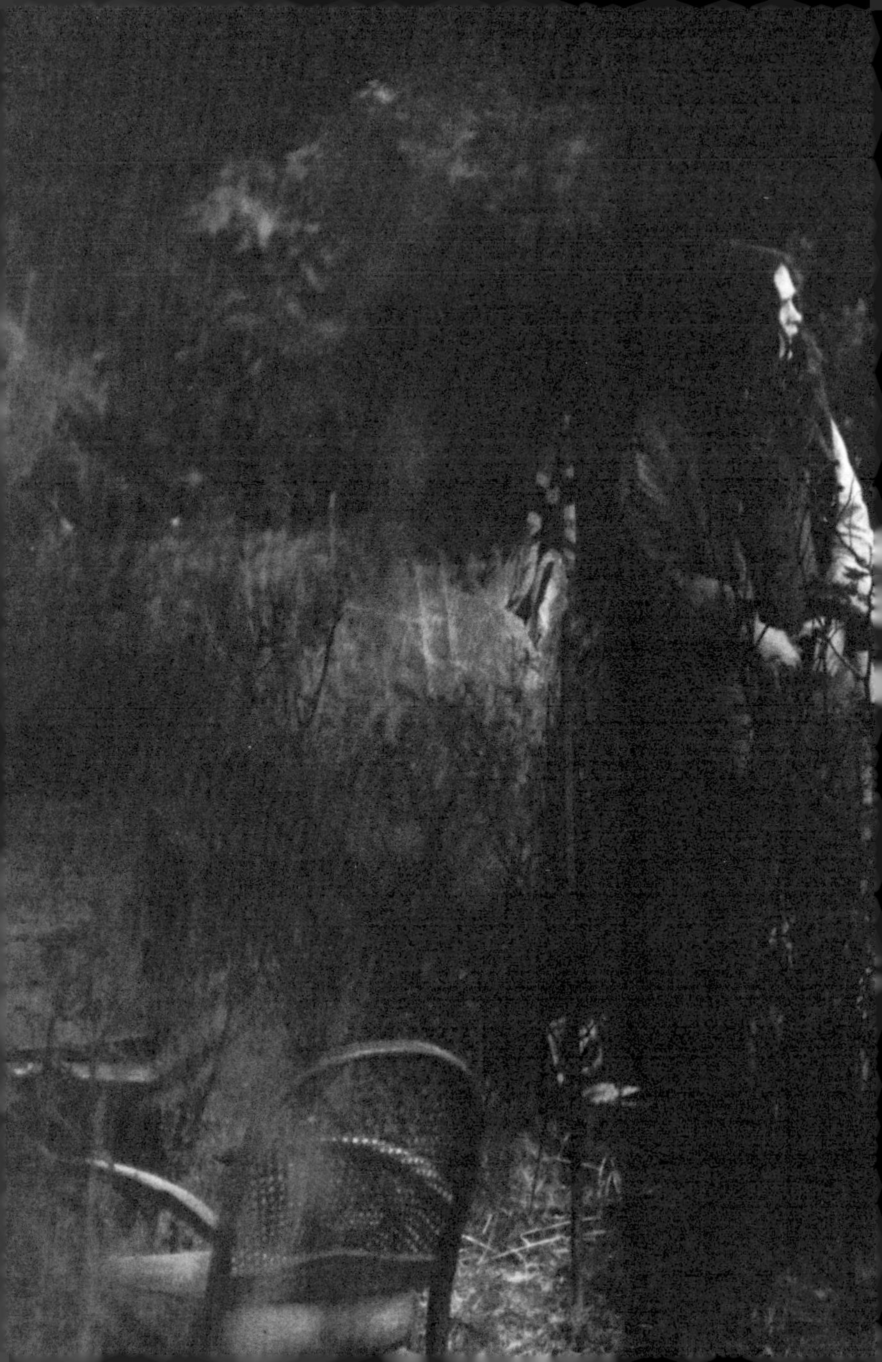

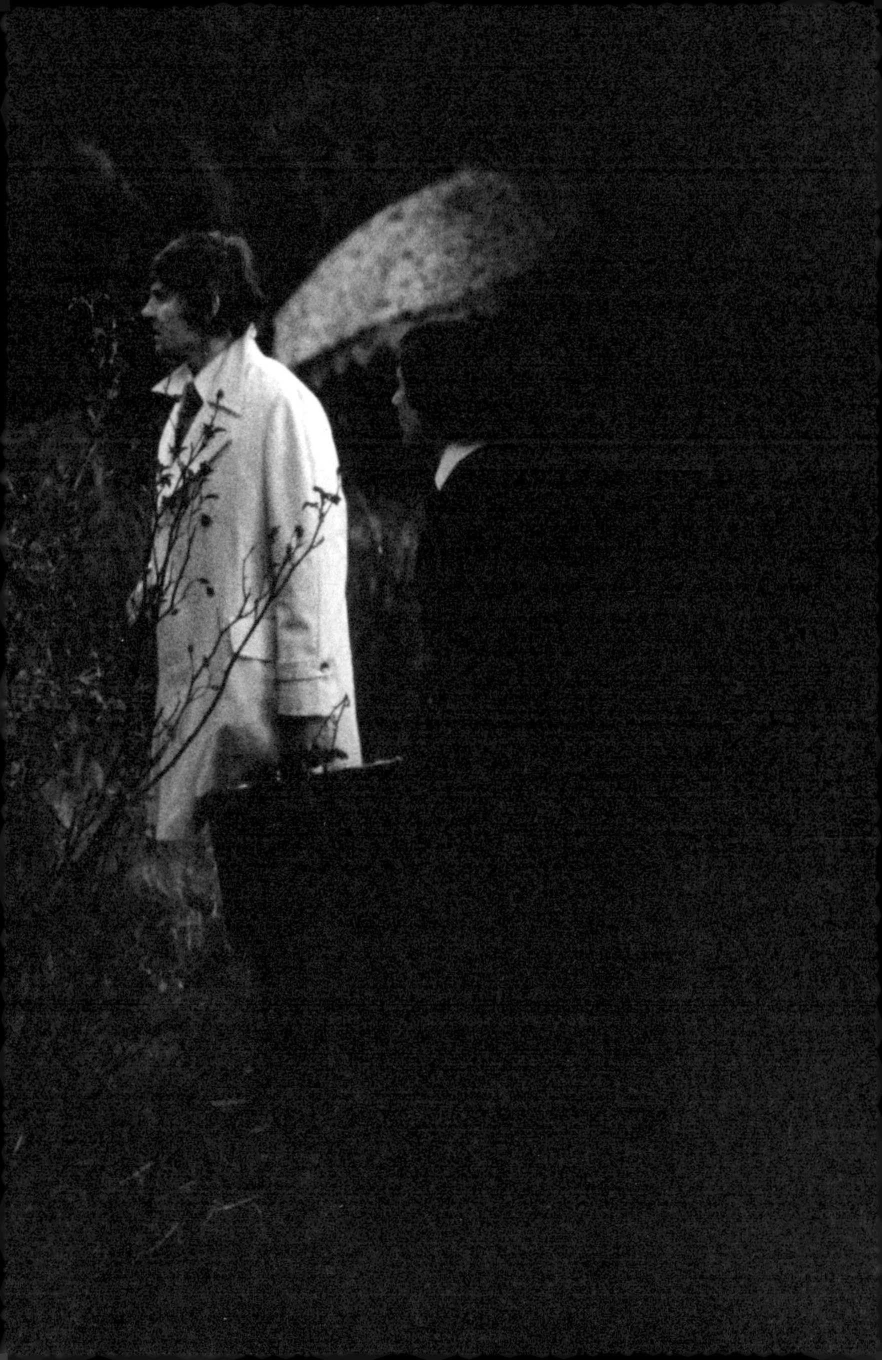

Confrontation with the Water Board, Bushey, Herts.

Hysteria, Luton.

Public telephones have started
to ring spontaneously.

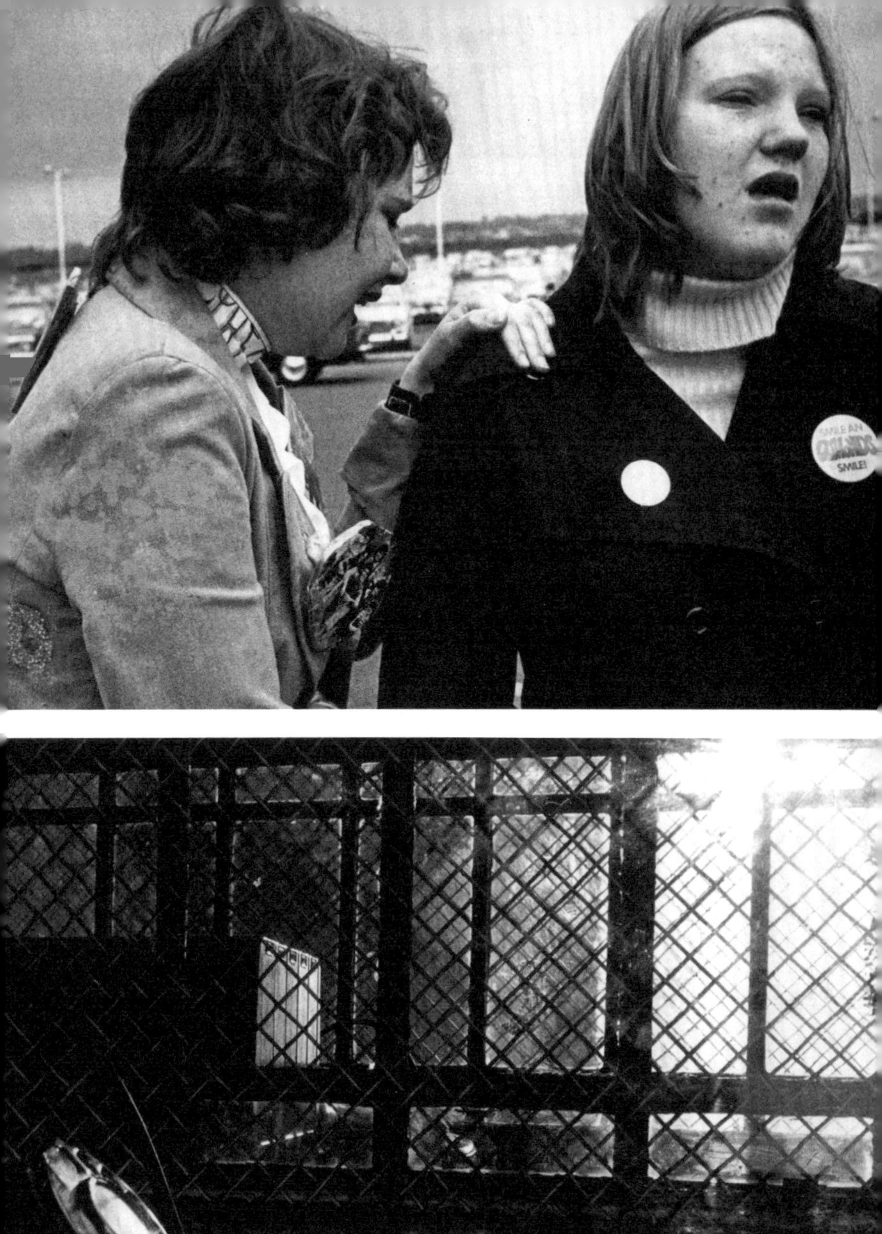
SMILE AN
SMILE!

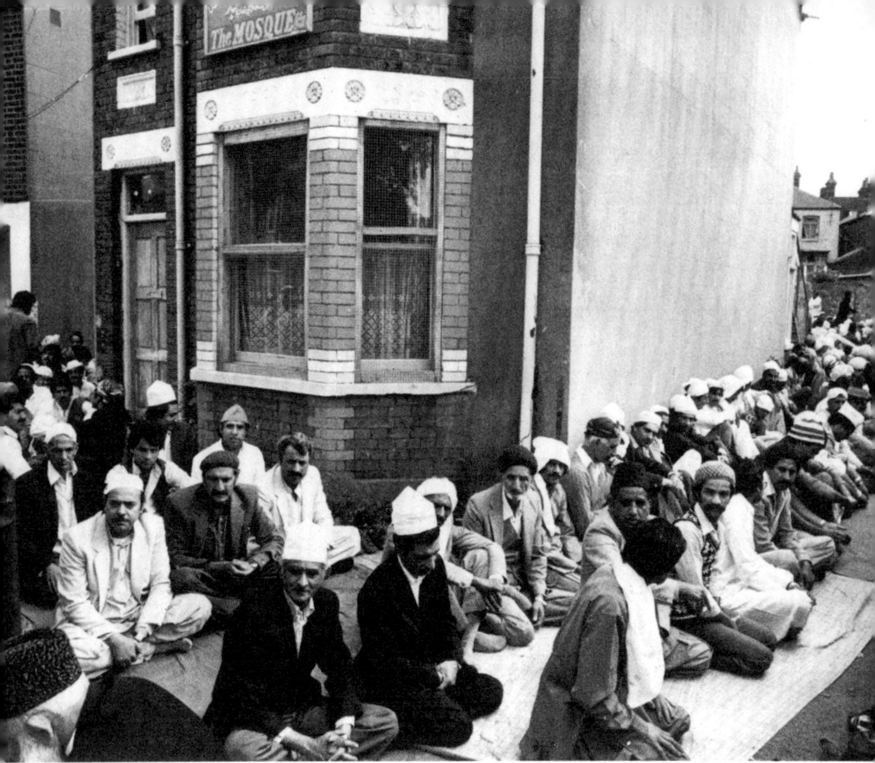

Group of adherents hold a vigil
in Westbourne Road, Luton.

Hitching gasworks.

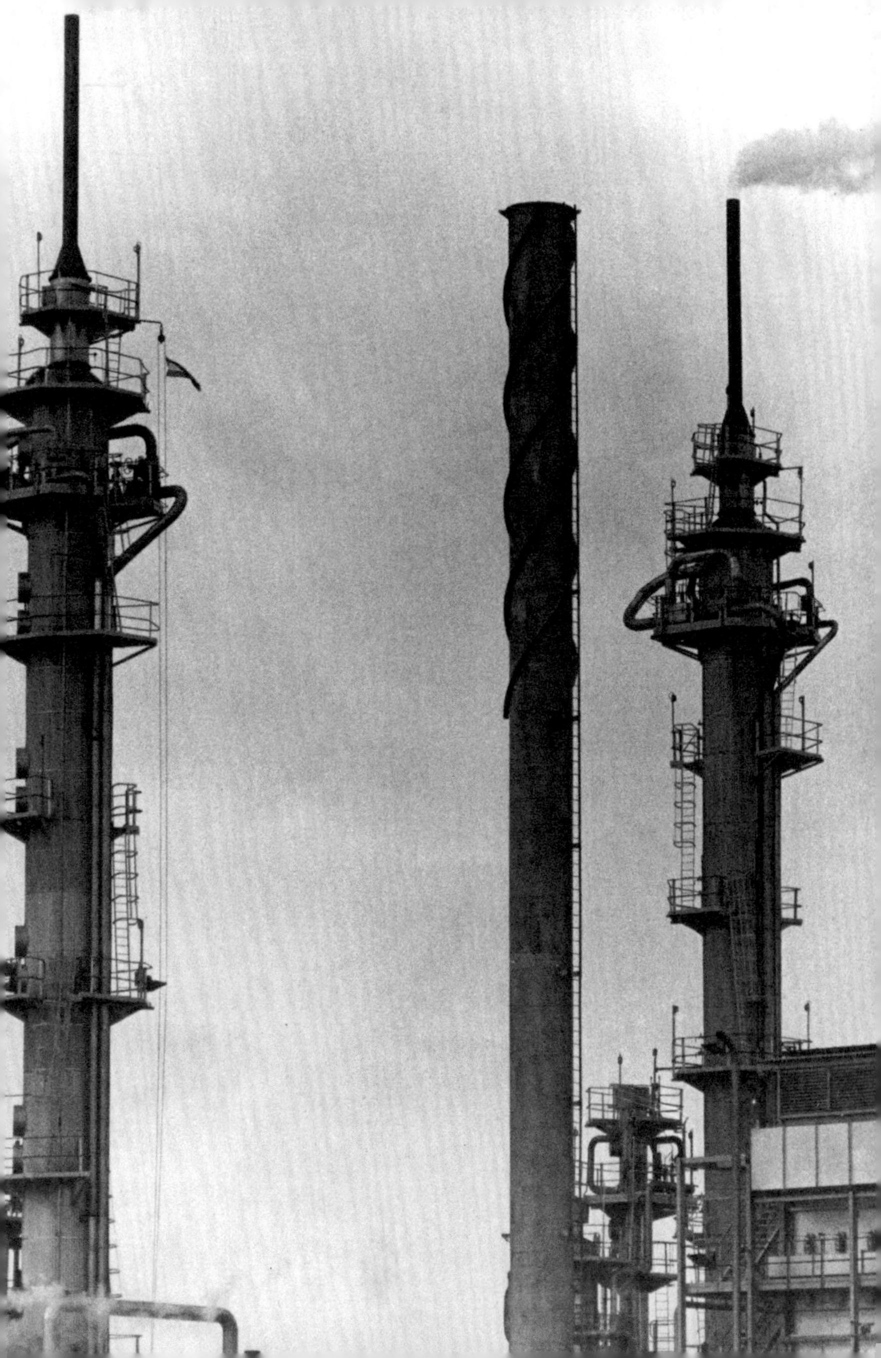

Meteor that went through a shop window at Blundell Street, Luton.

Minister at Little Gaddesden turns a blind eye to the fears of the young.

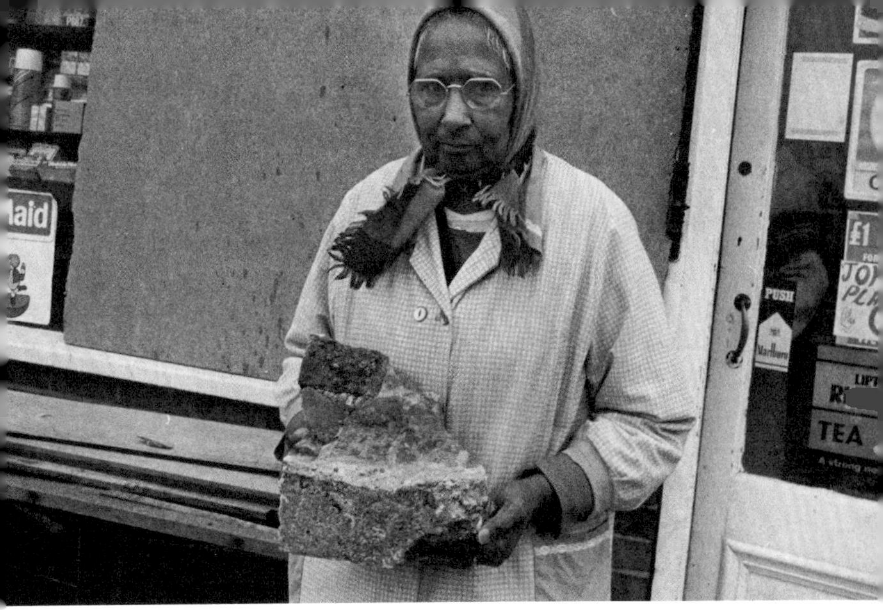

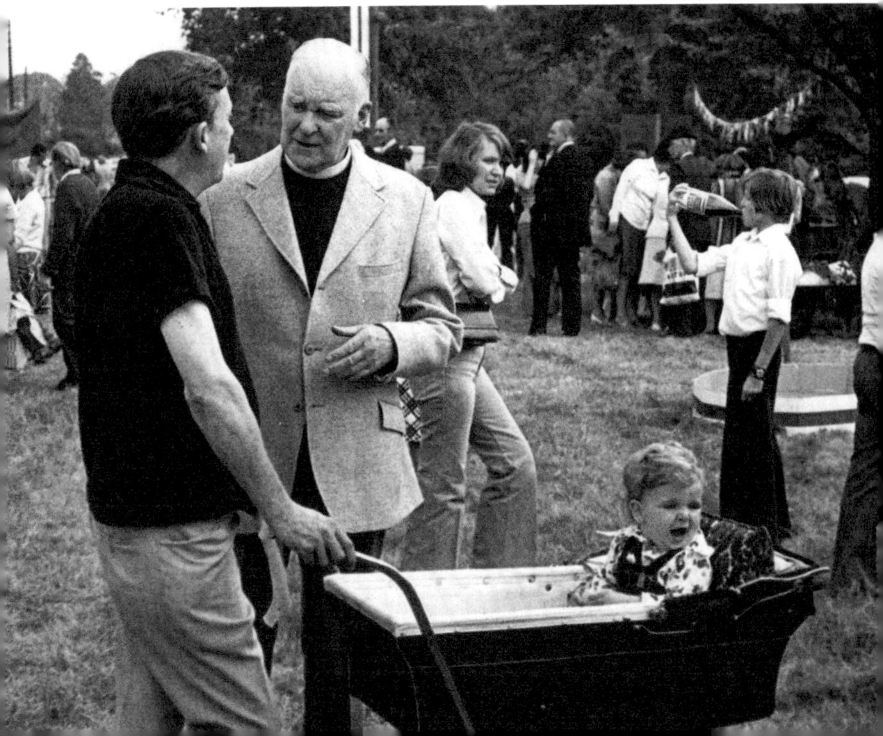

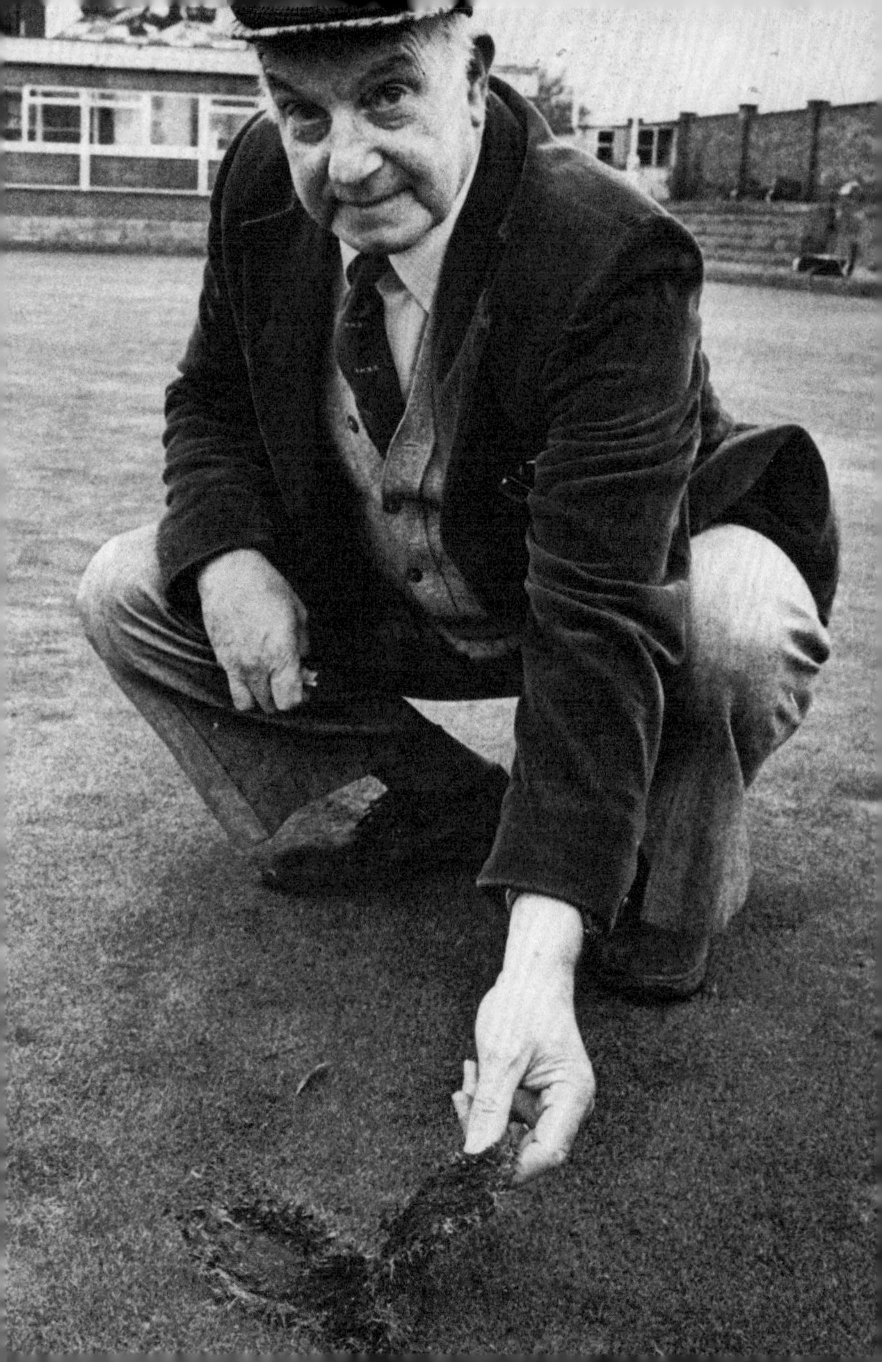

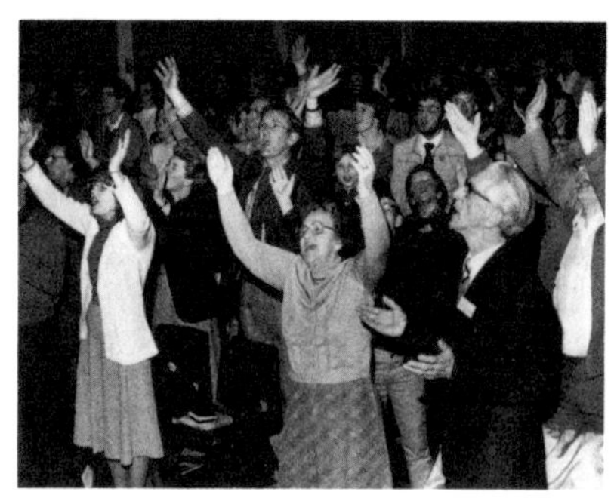

Kingdom Life crusade at Hemel Hempstead.

A sign in the earth at Beech Hill, Luton.

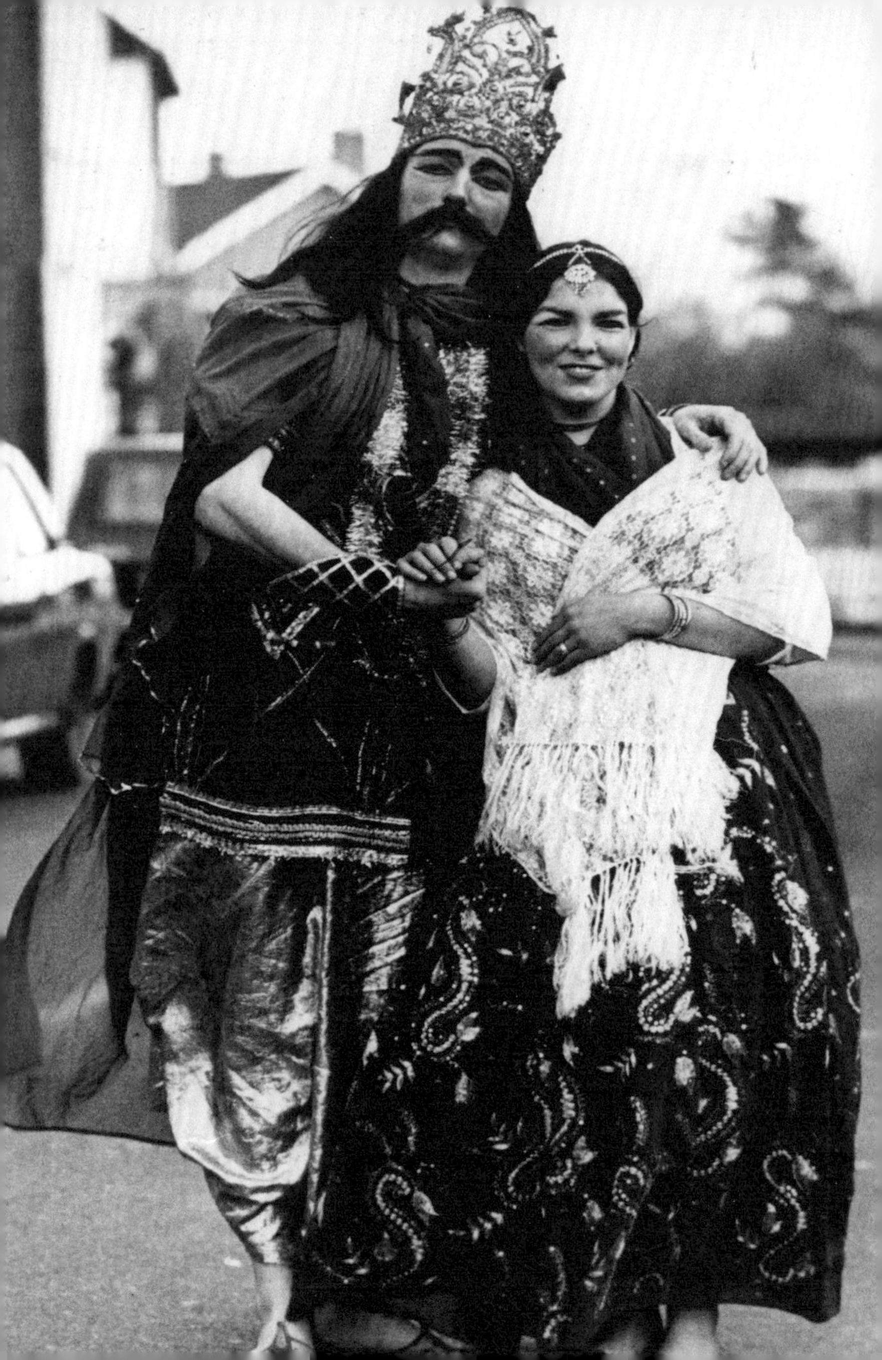

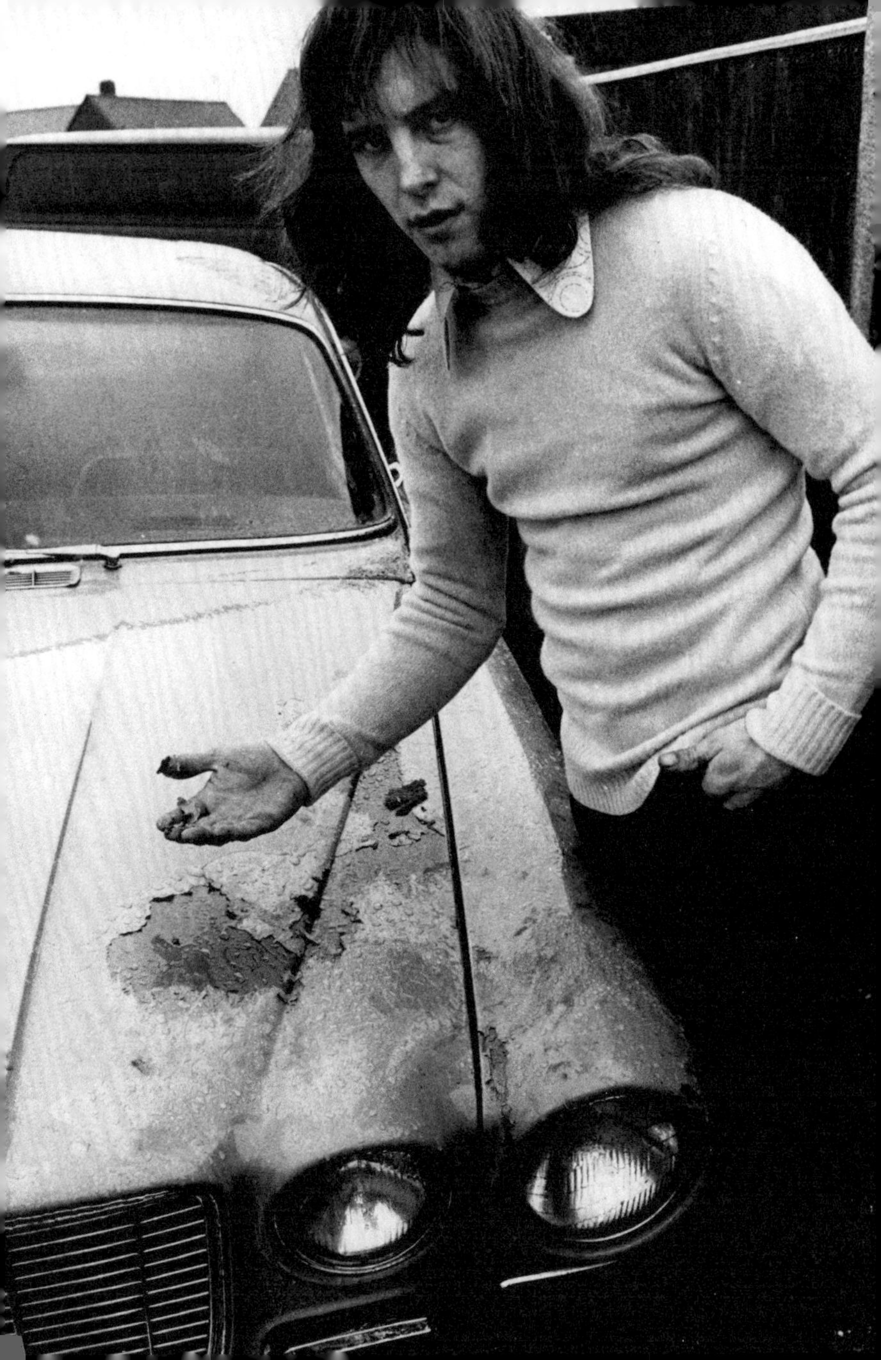

Spurious kings are becoming a
problem at this end of times.

Brian examines a sign on his car.

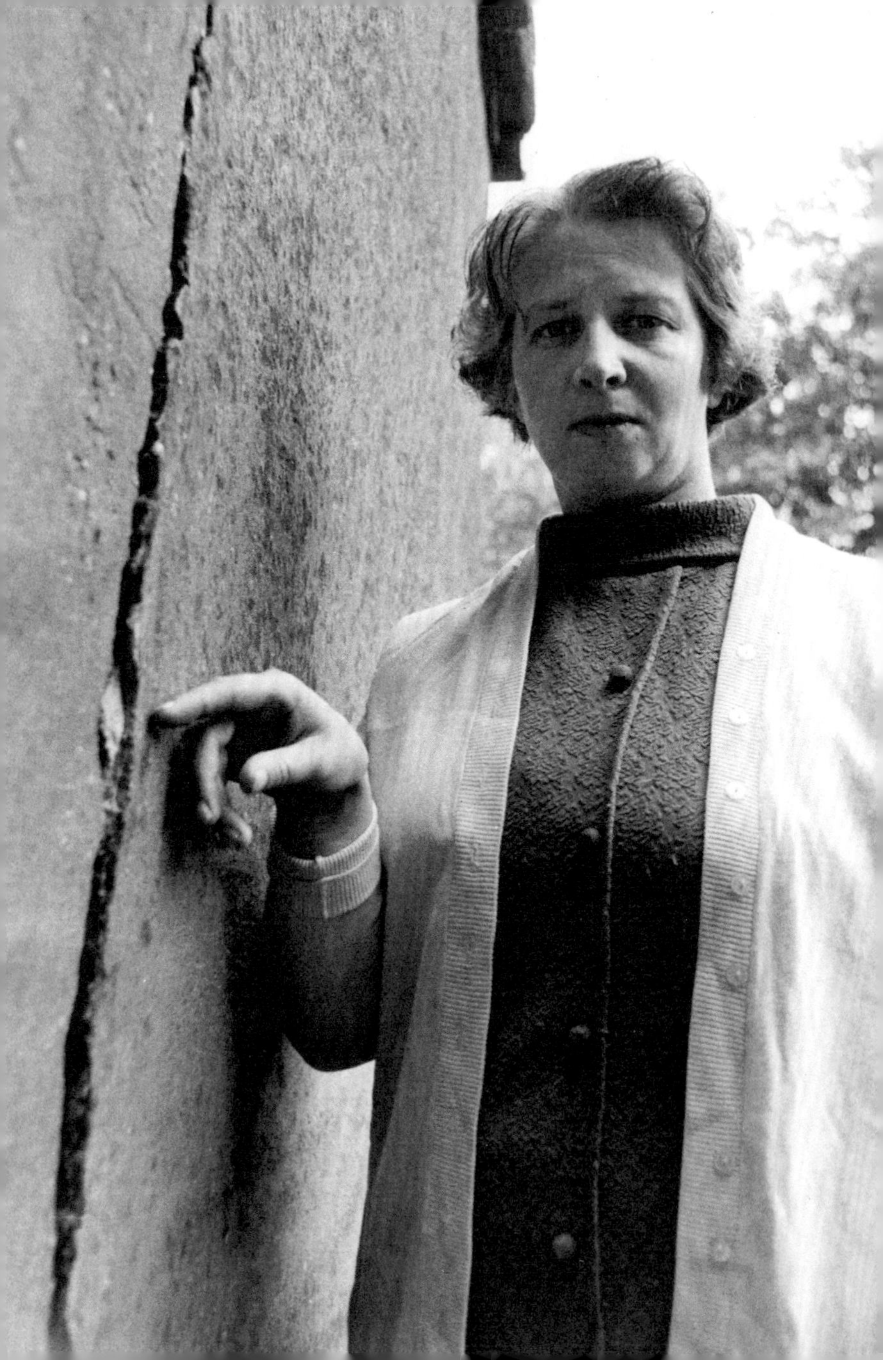

Mrs Palmer examines a sign in Scrubbitts Square, Radlett.

Broken angels.

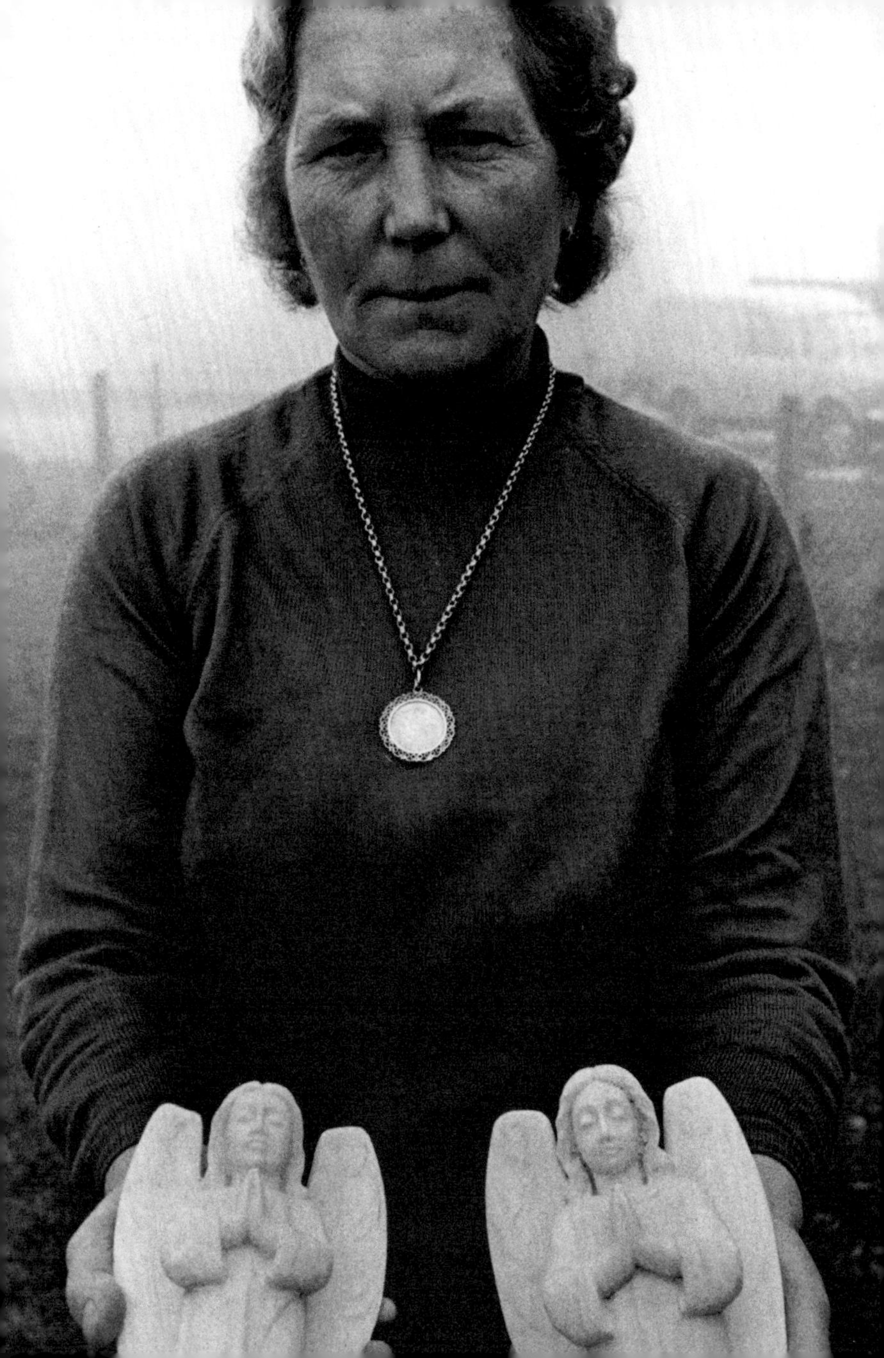

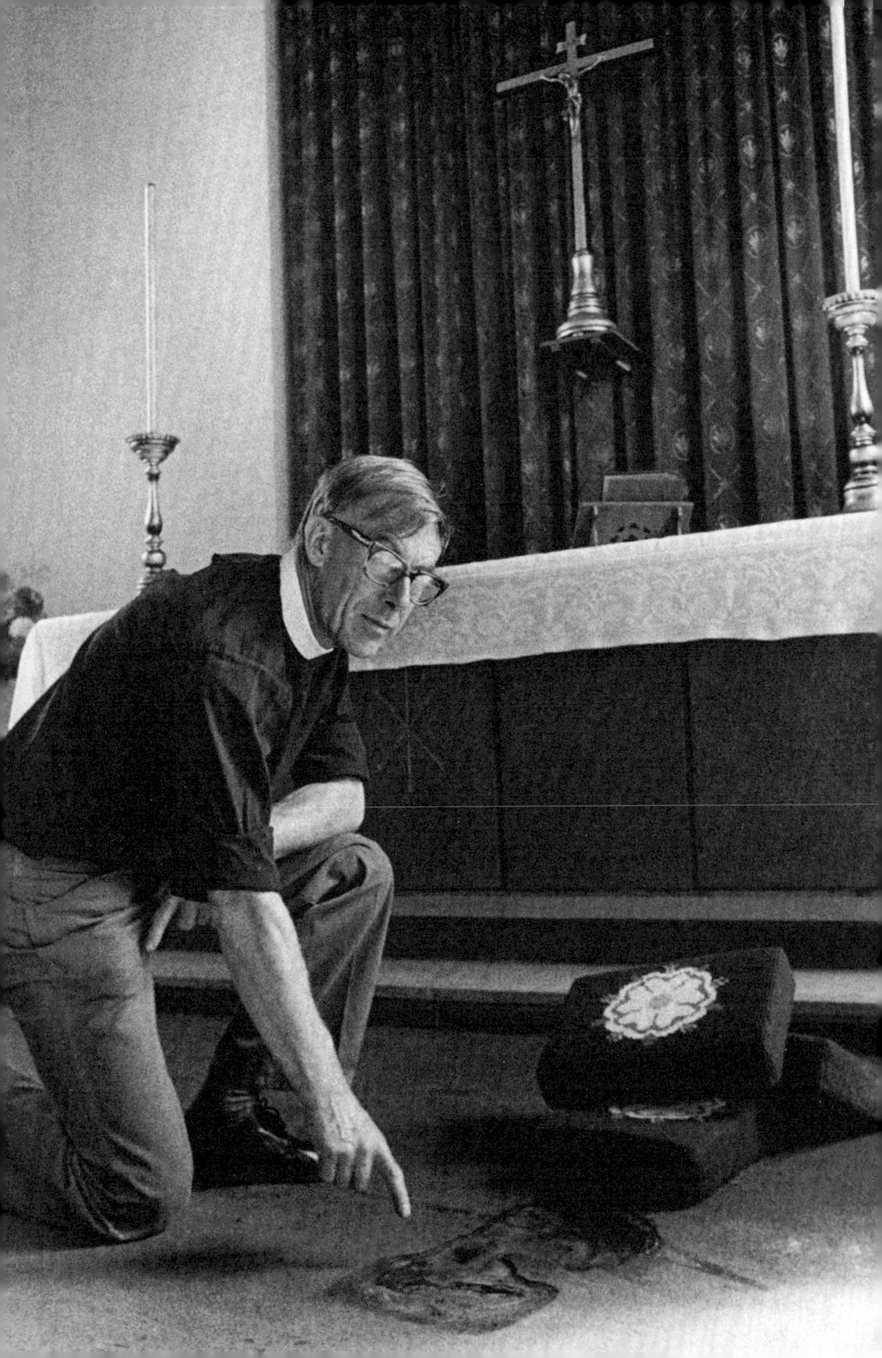

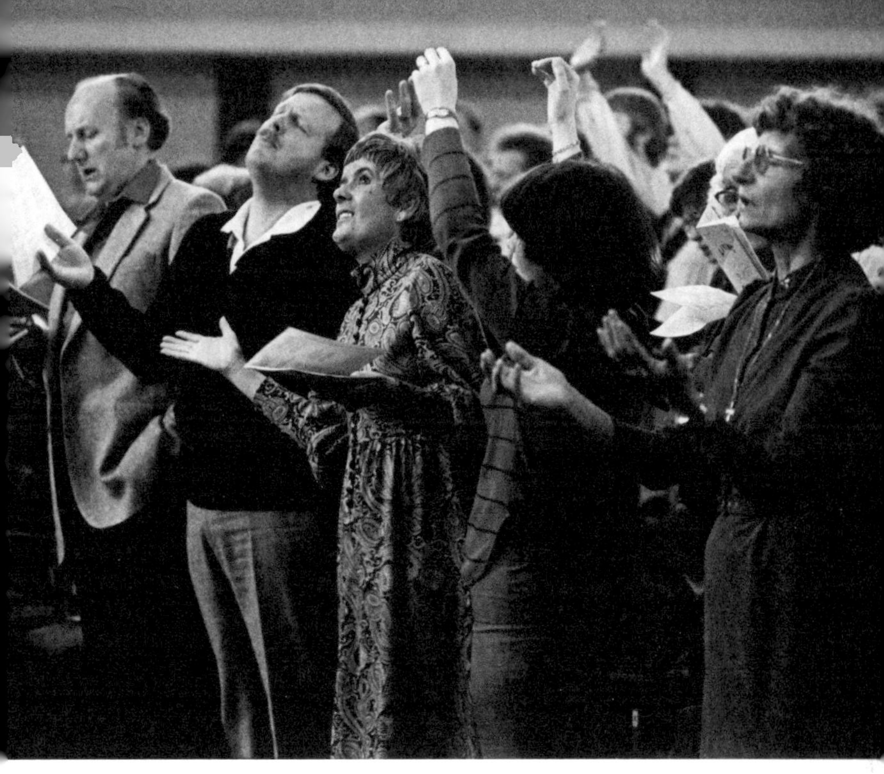

The faithful congregation praise a mystery.

A sign at Warners End Church. The Reverend Fletcher examines the water damage.

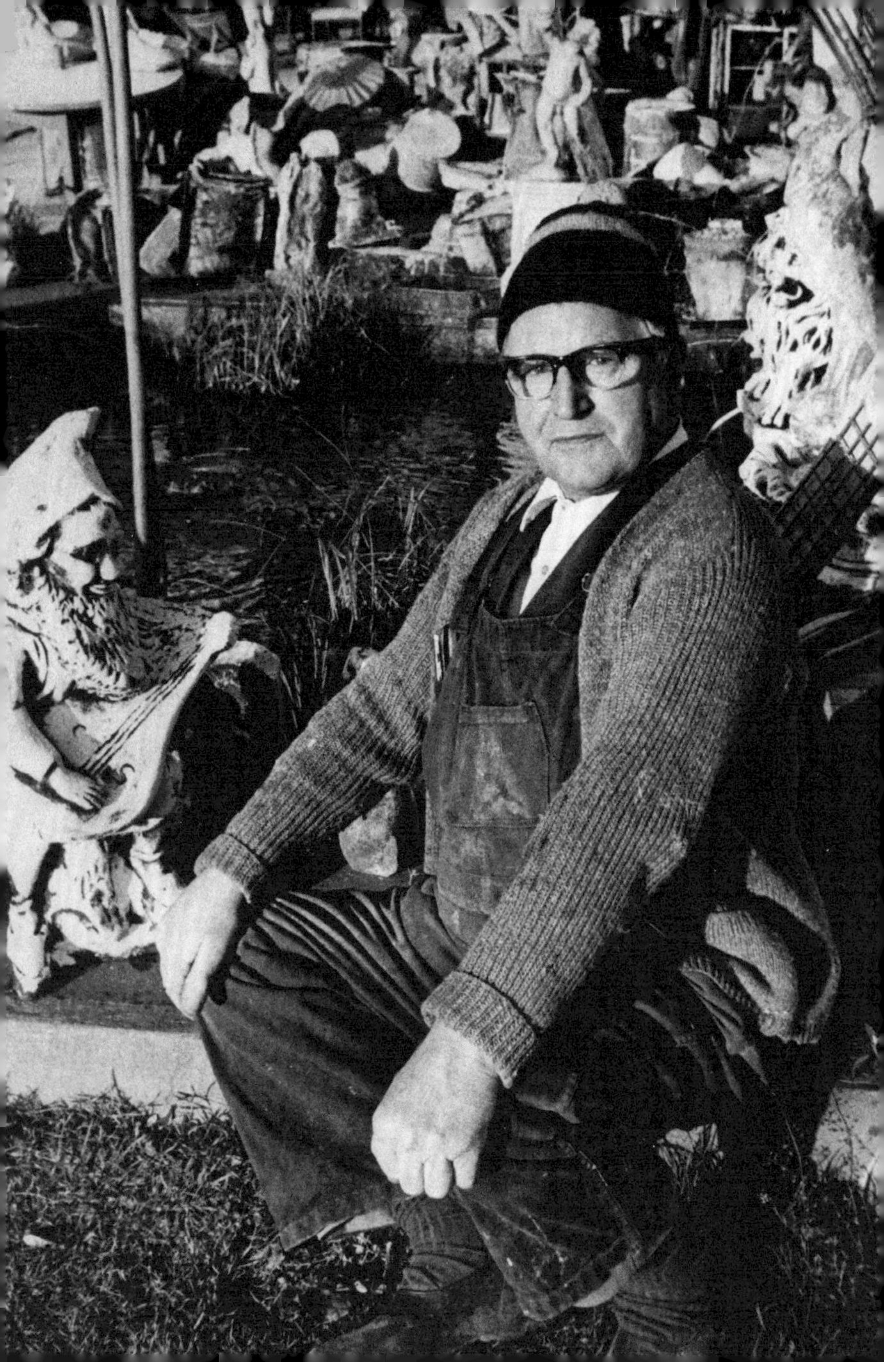

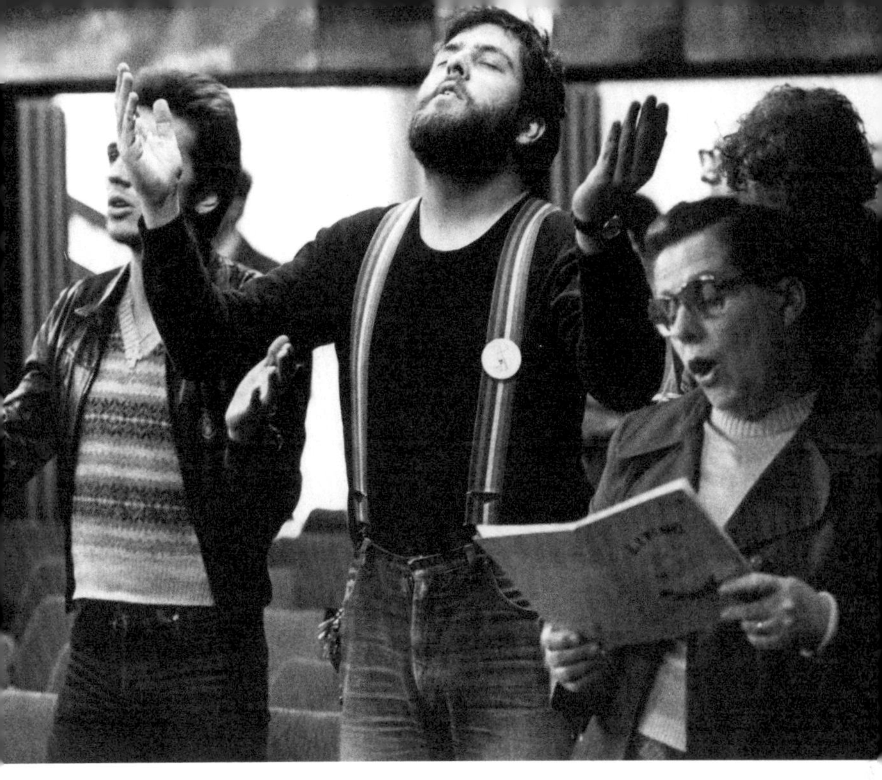

New congregations are born every day in Hemel.

New prophet Robert King has many followers.

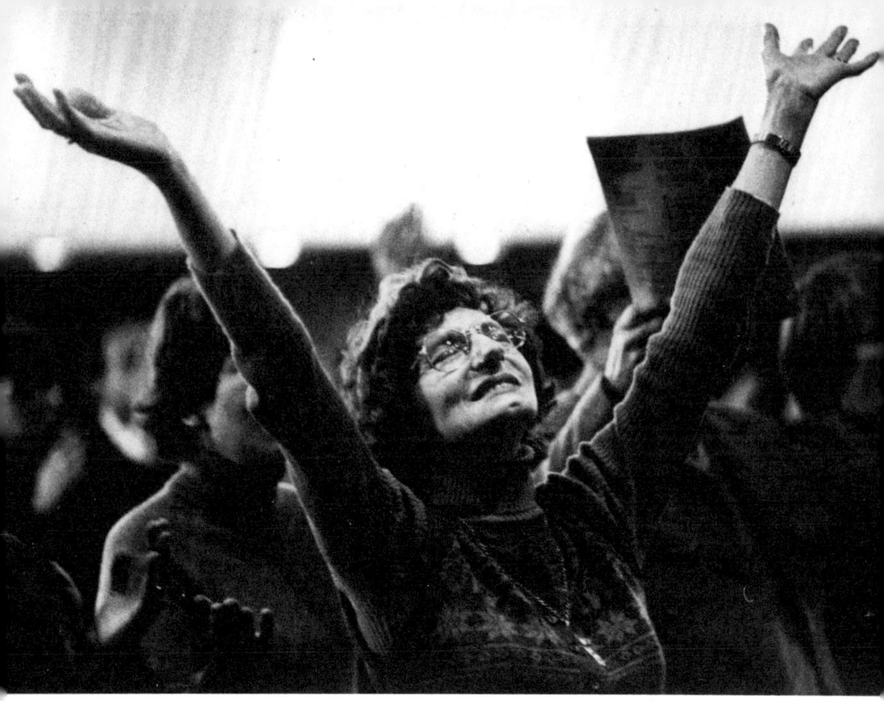

"Lord of Chaos" congregation
last night.

Prophetess Doris Browne, Luton.

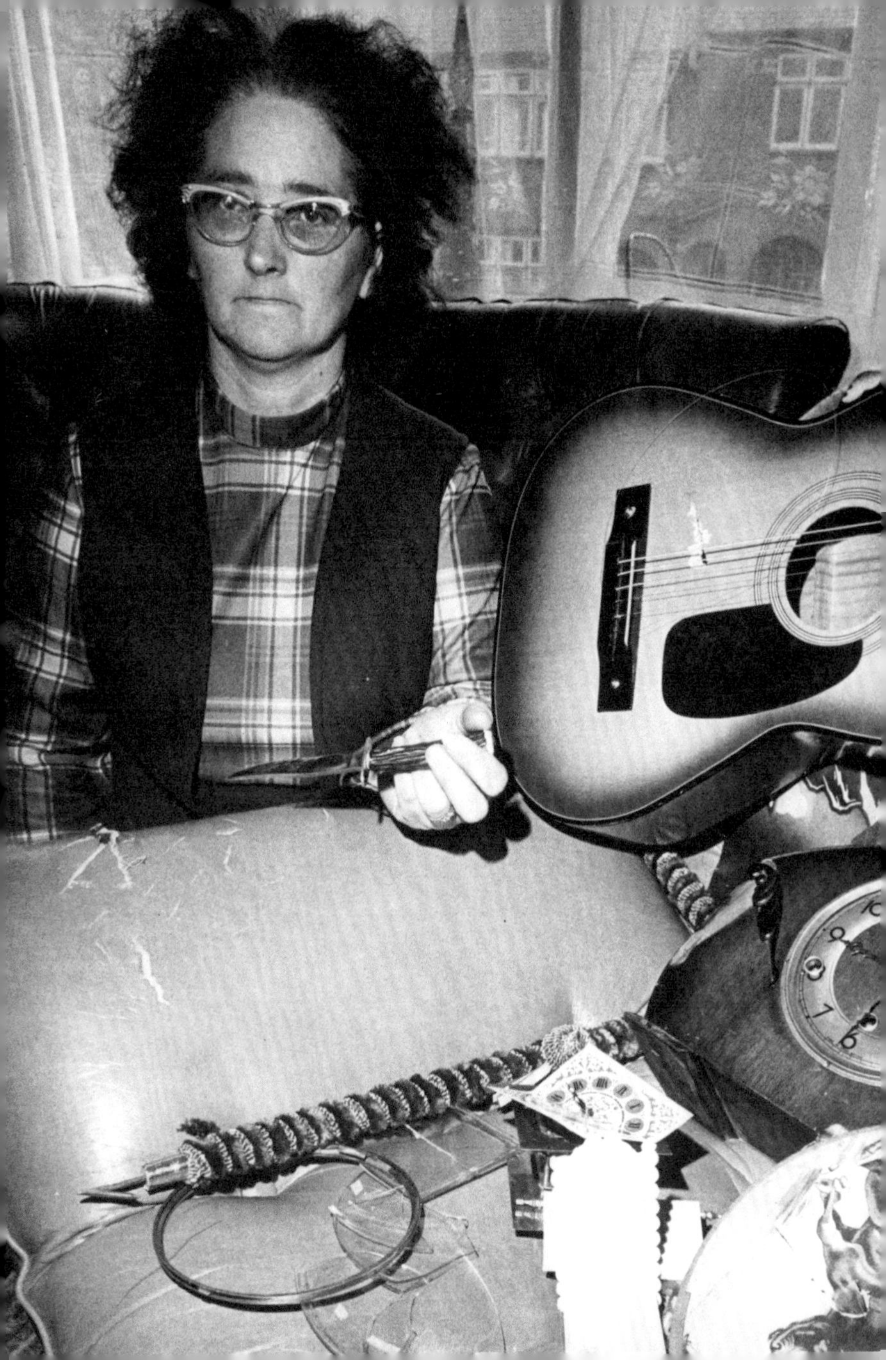

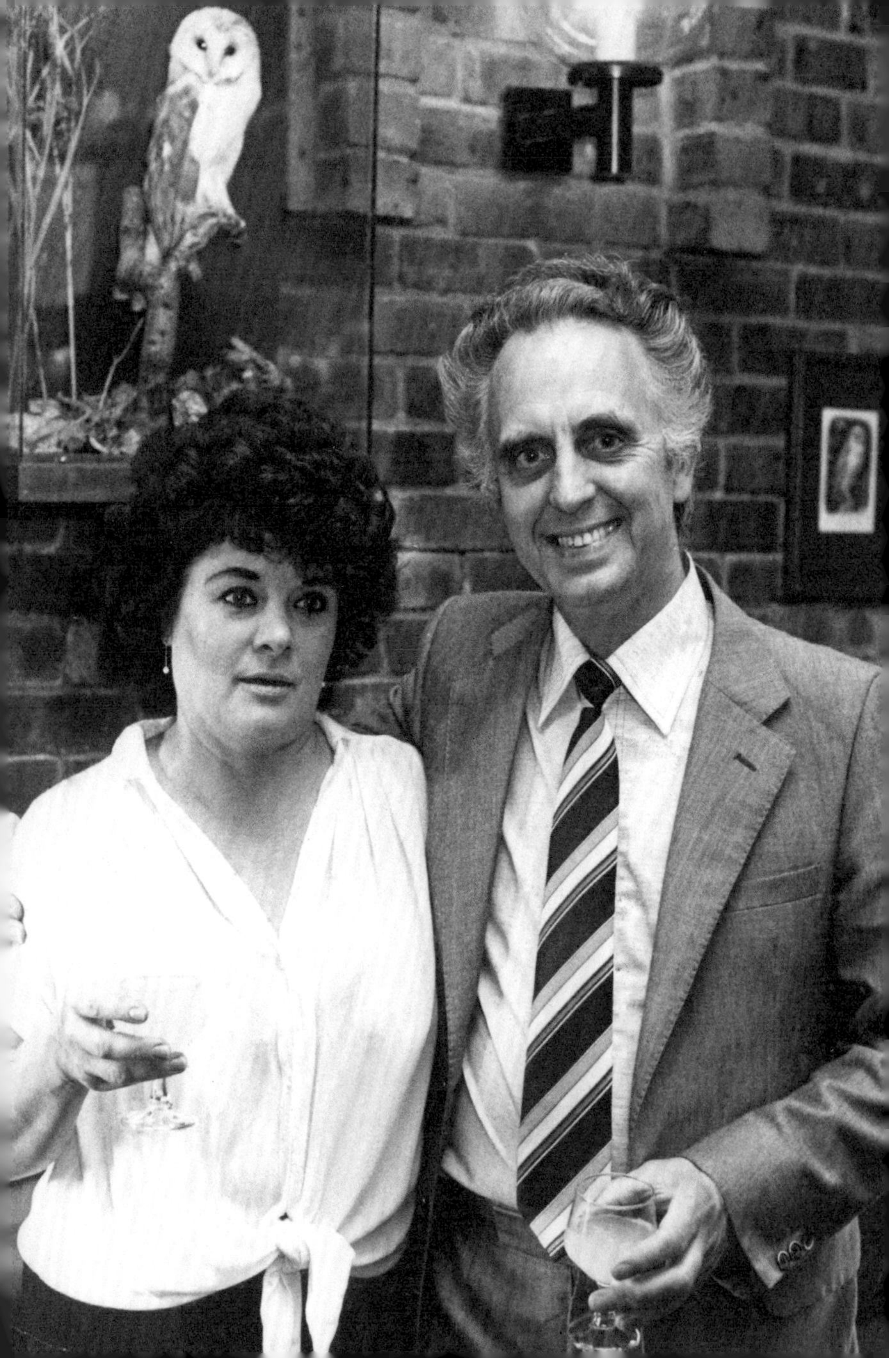

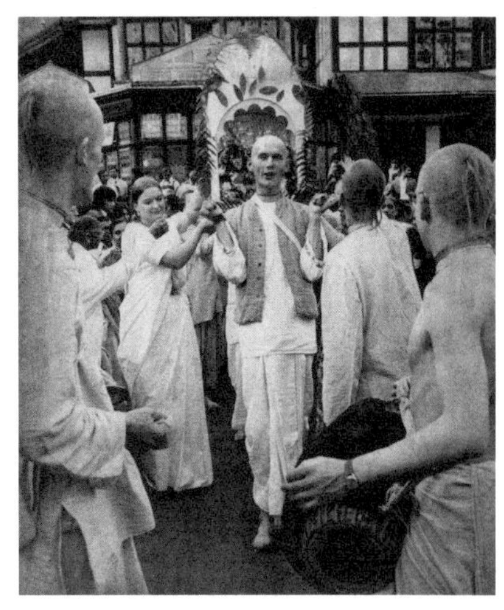

Hairless bird prophet, Letchmore Heath.

Beverley and Jim in the Barn Owl Chapel, Caddington.

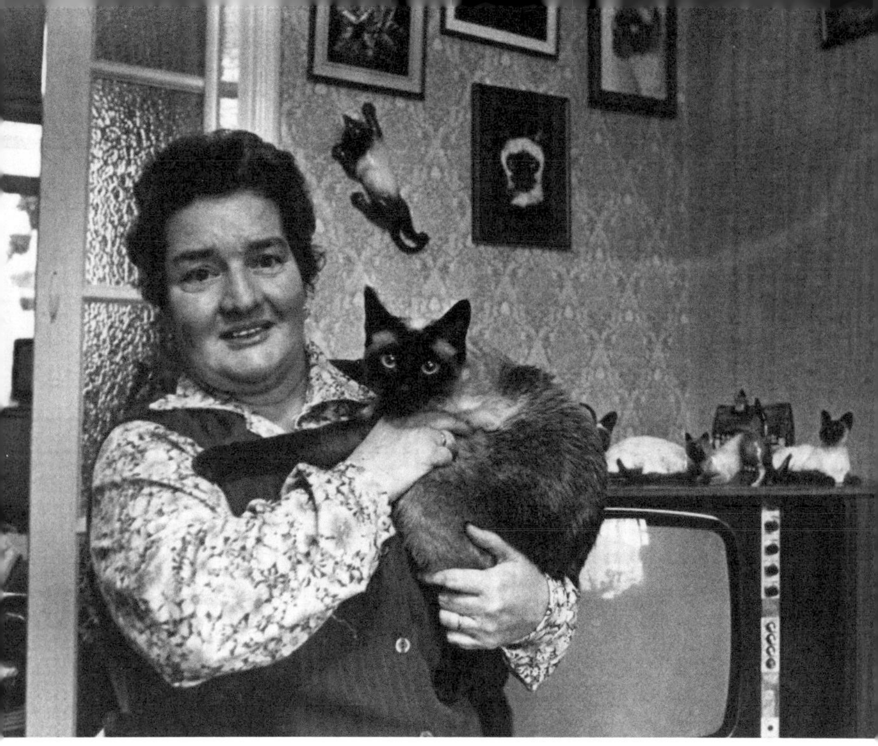

The old believers are witnessing
a massive revival.

Dancing at cat festivities.

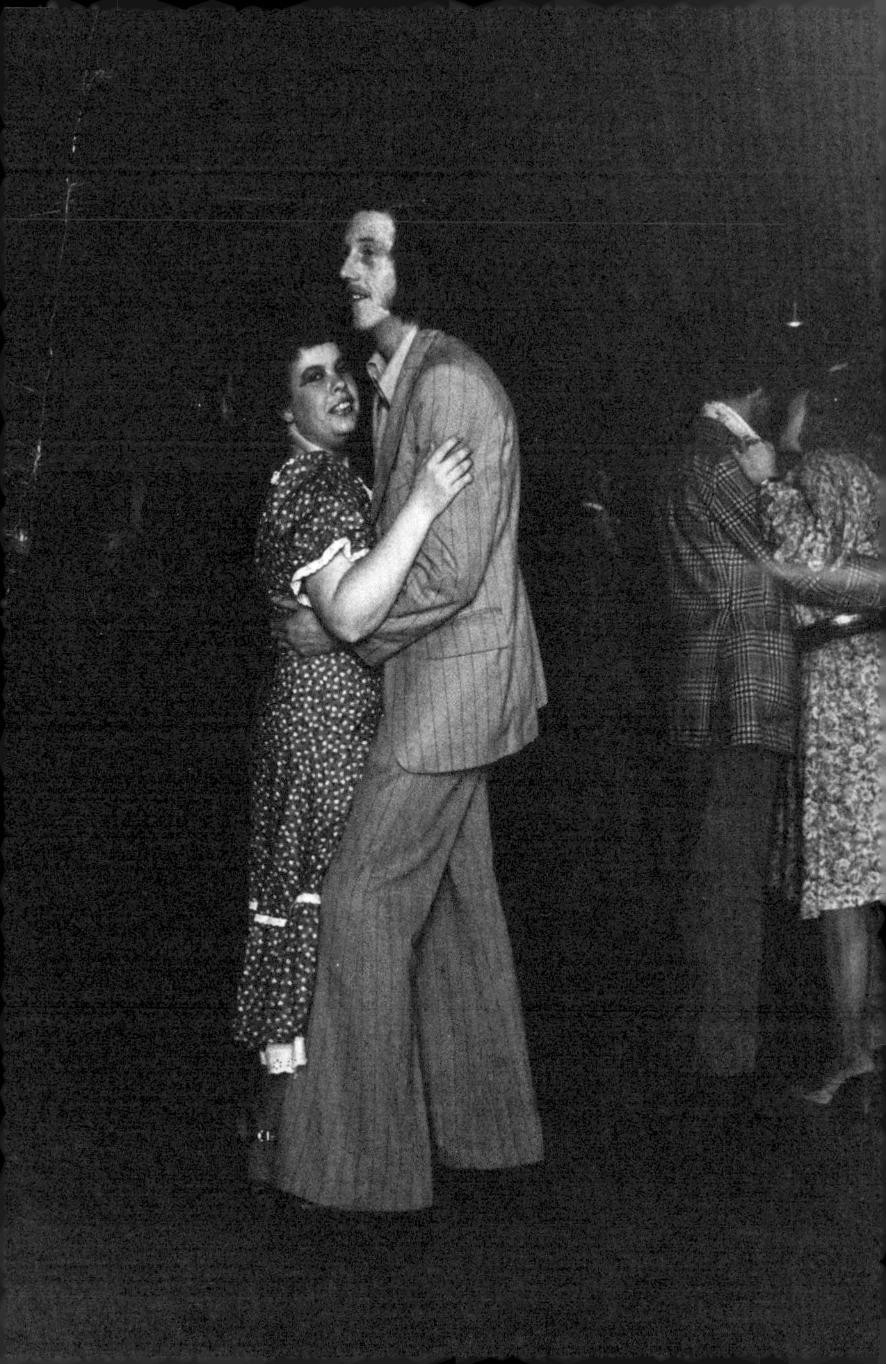

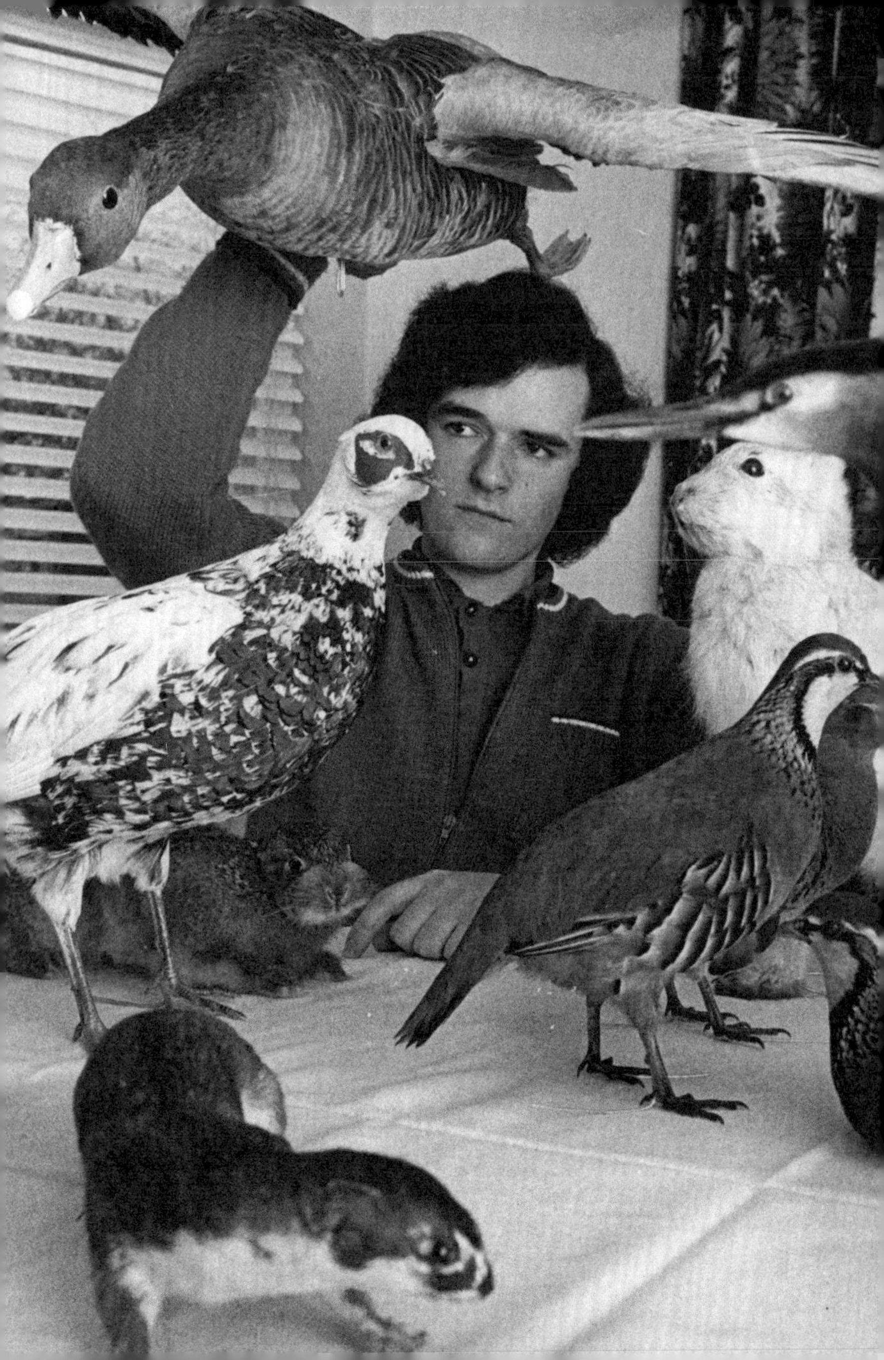

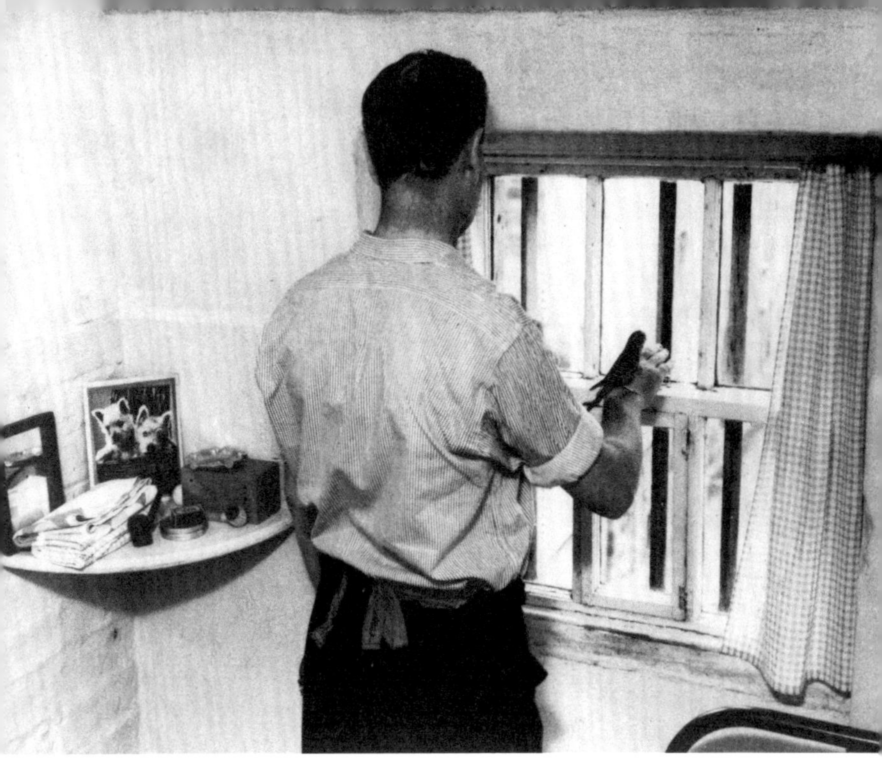

Man and bird in barred window ecstasy.

Prophet Martin Adams.

Linmere School, Houghton Regis.

Adoration of the broken windows.

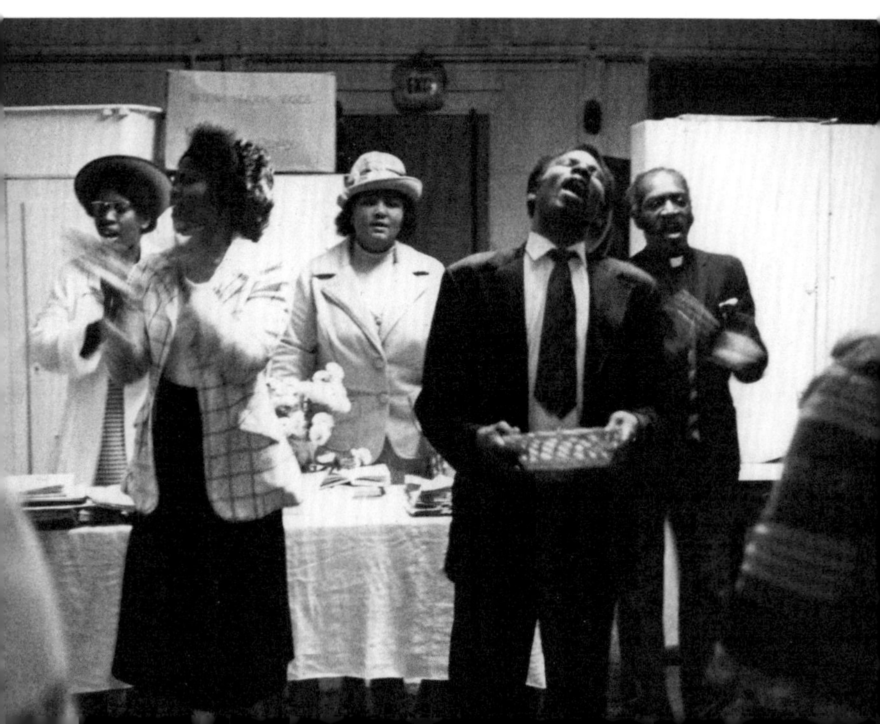

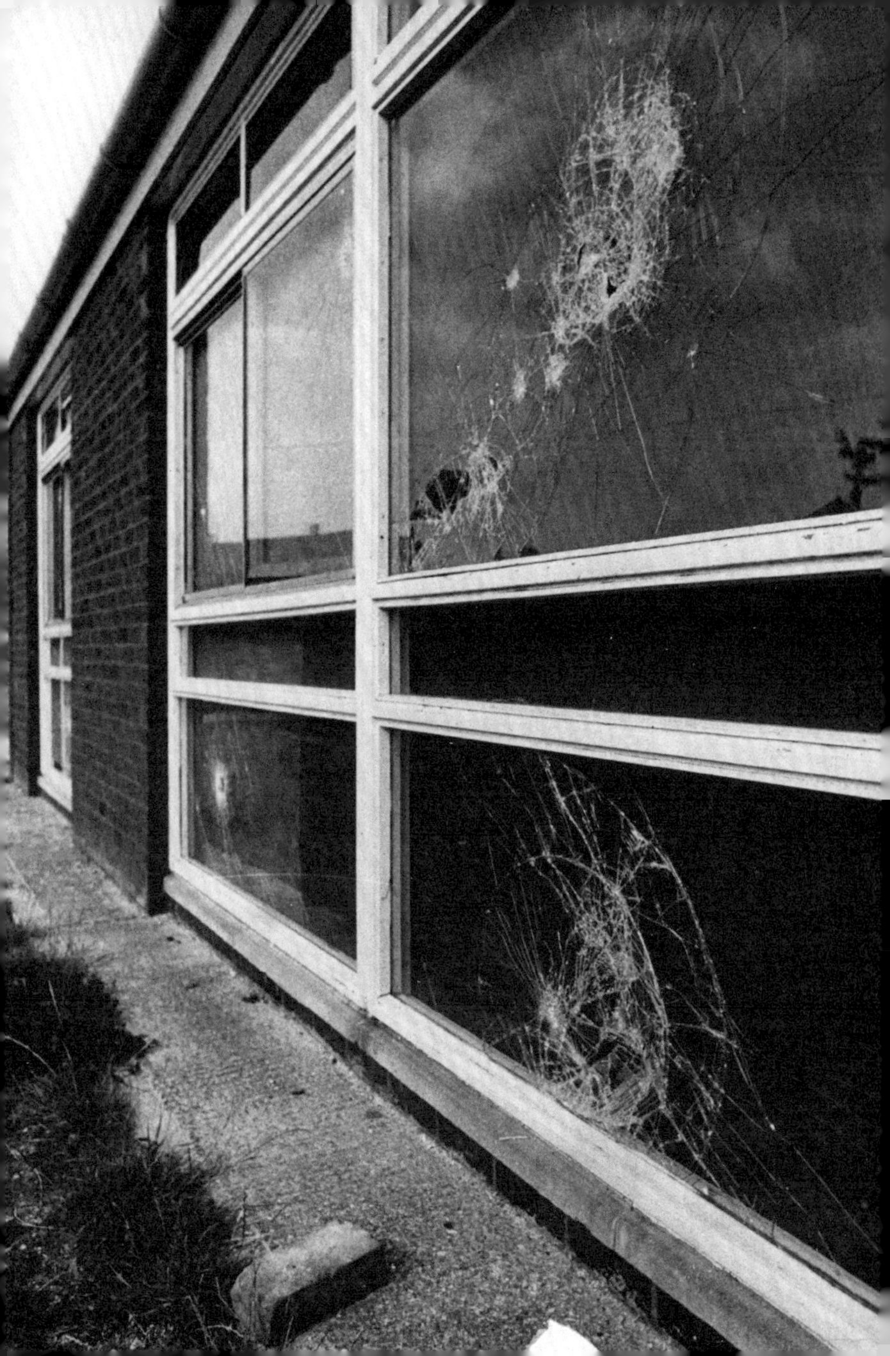

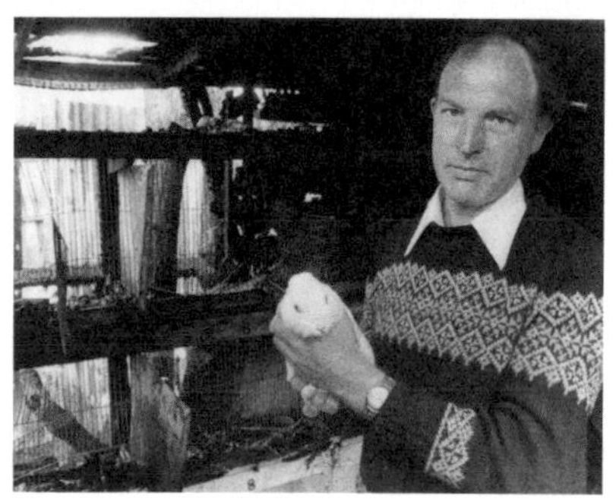

Mr Barry Boyce explains the situation to one of his rabbits.

Bushey squatter from one of the Boyce congregations.

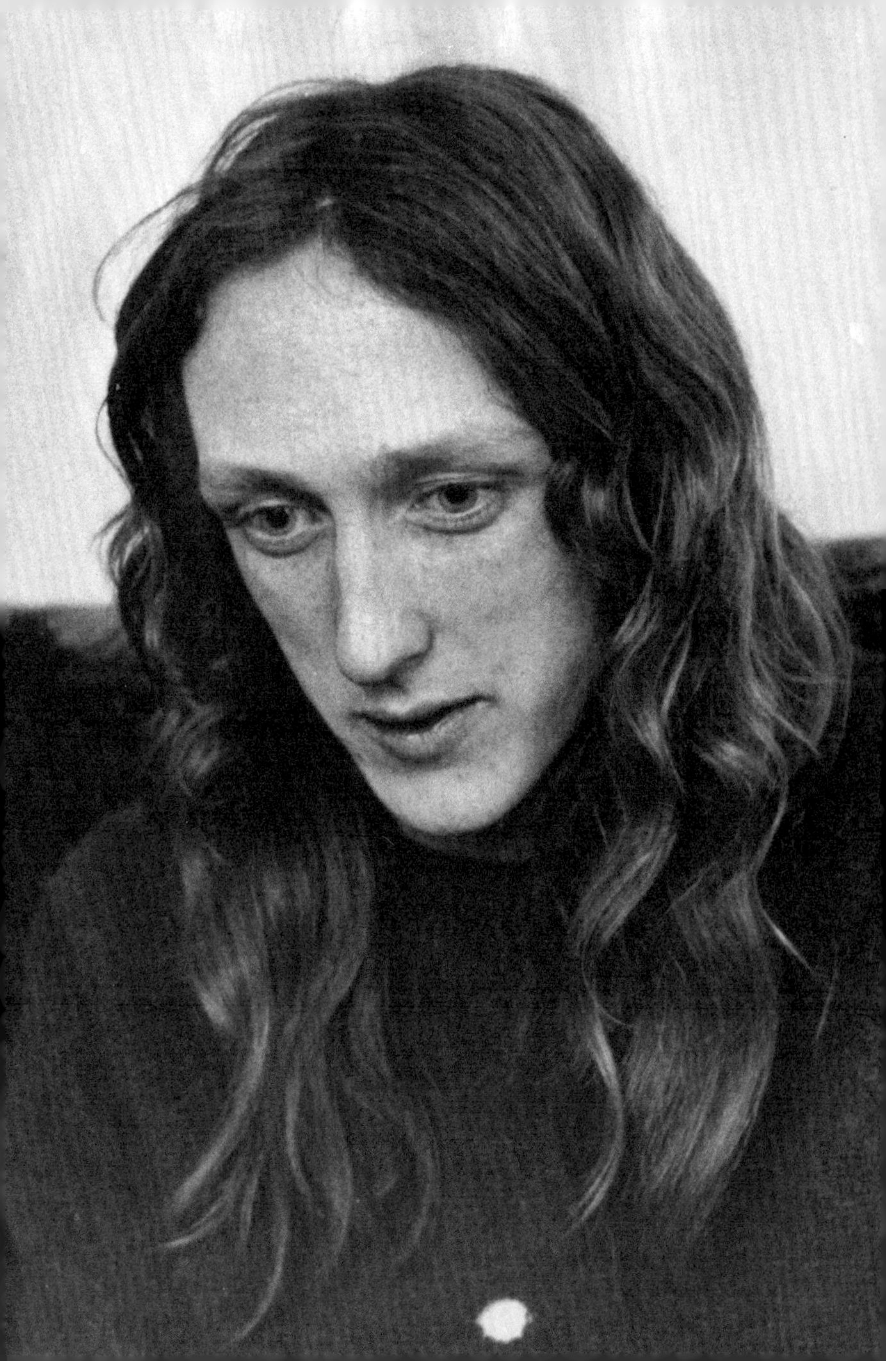

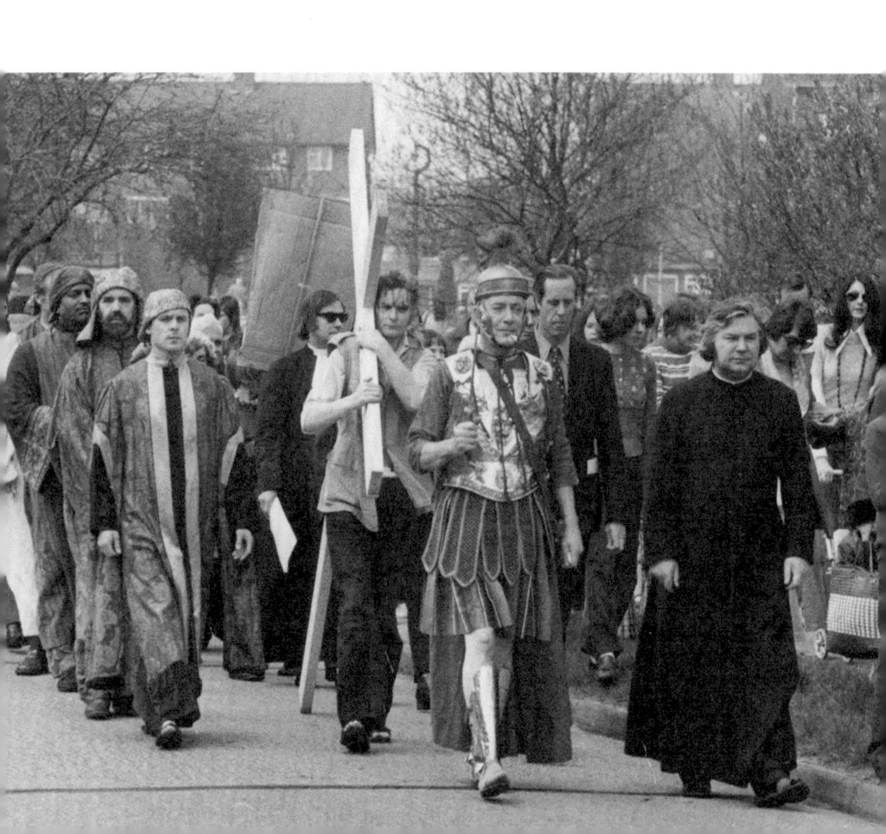

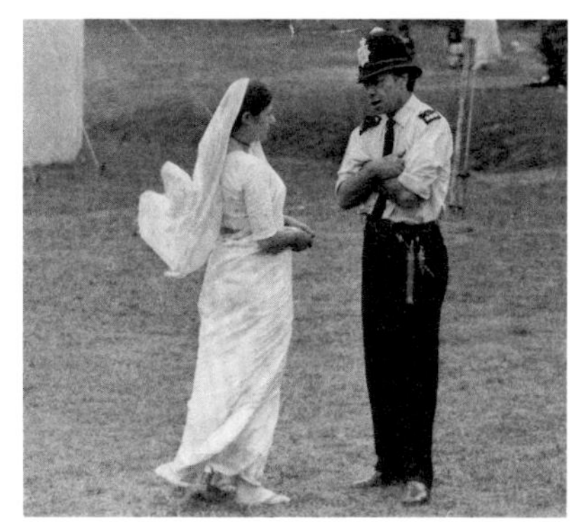

An angel speaks to PC Harry Mitchell.

Tony Elvidge professes to be the Chosen One.

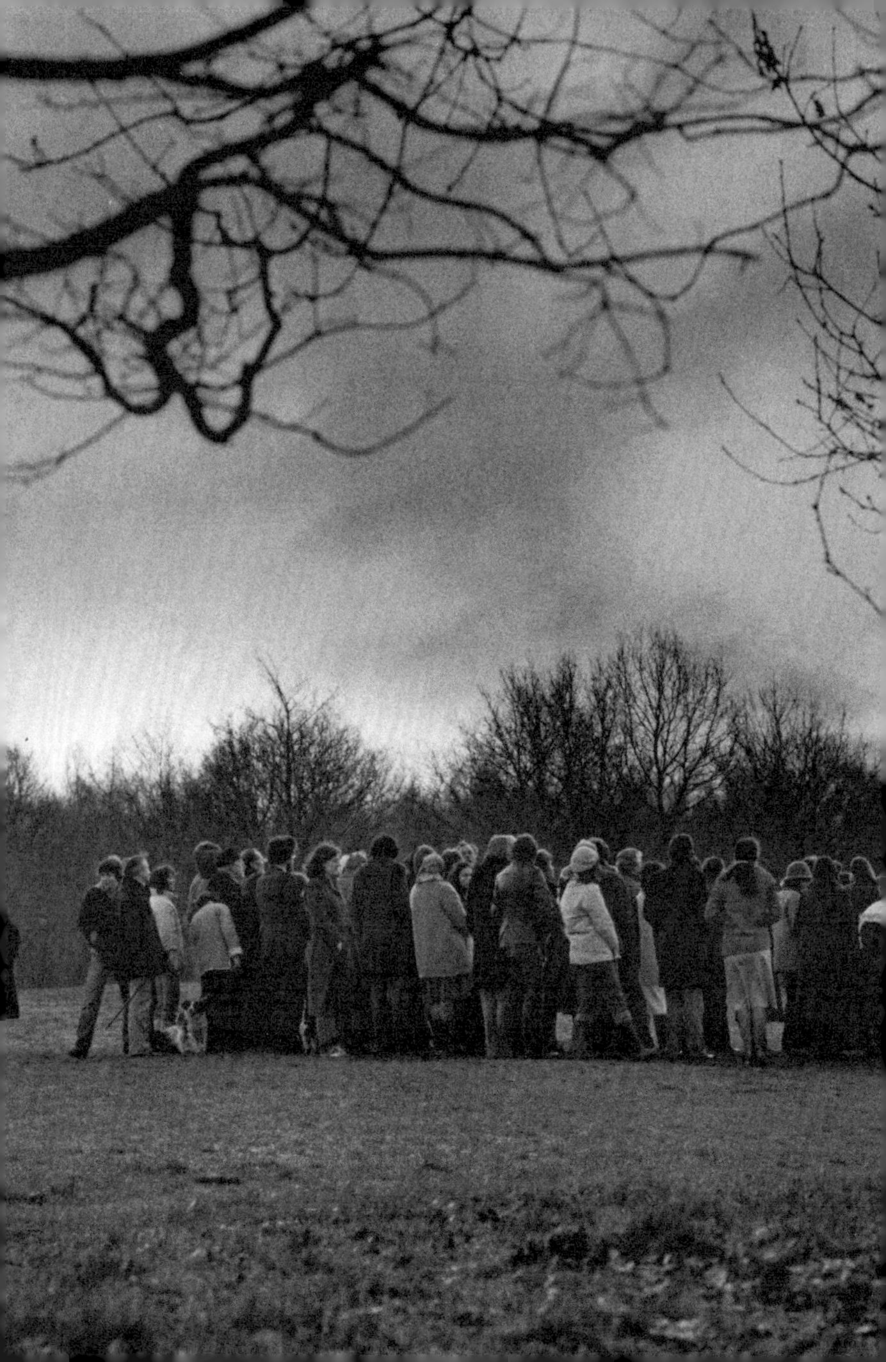

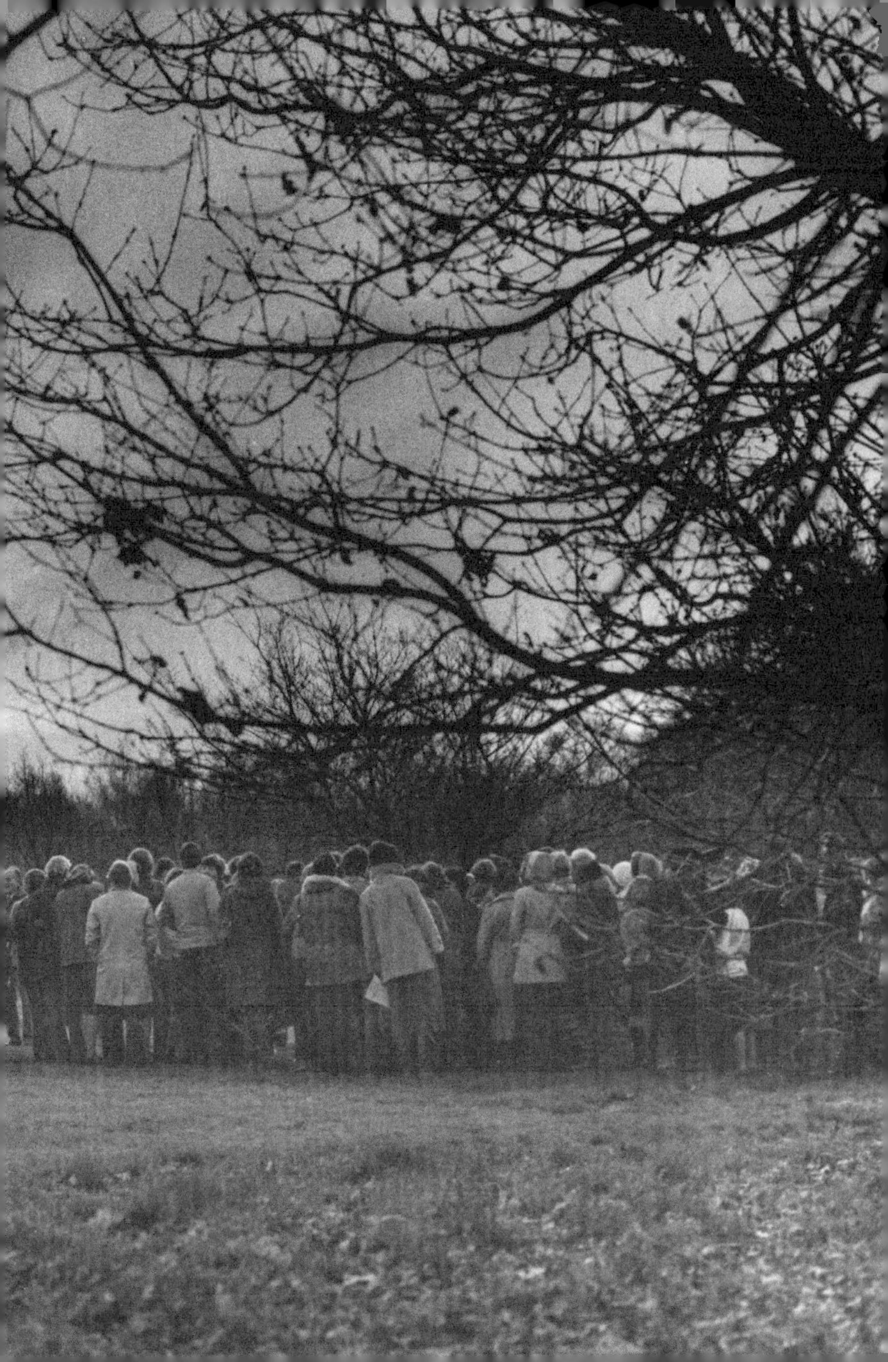

Chorleywood Common, prayers.

The sign of the broken glass,
Sedgewick Road, Luton.

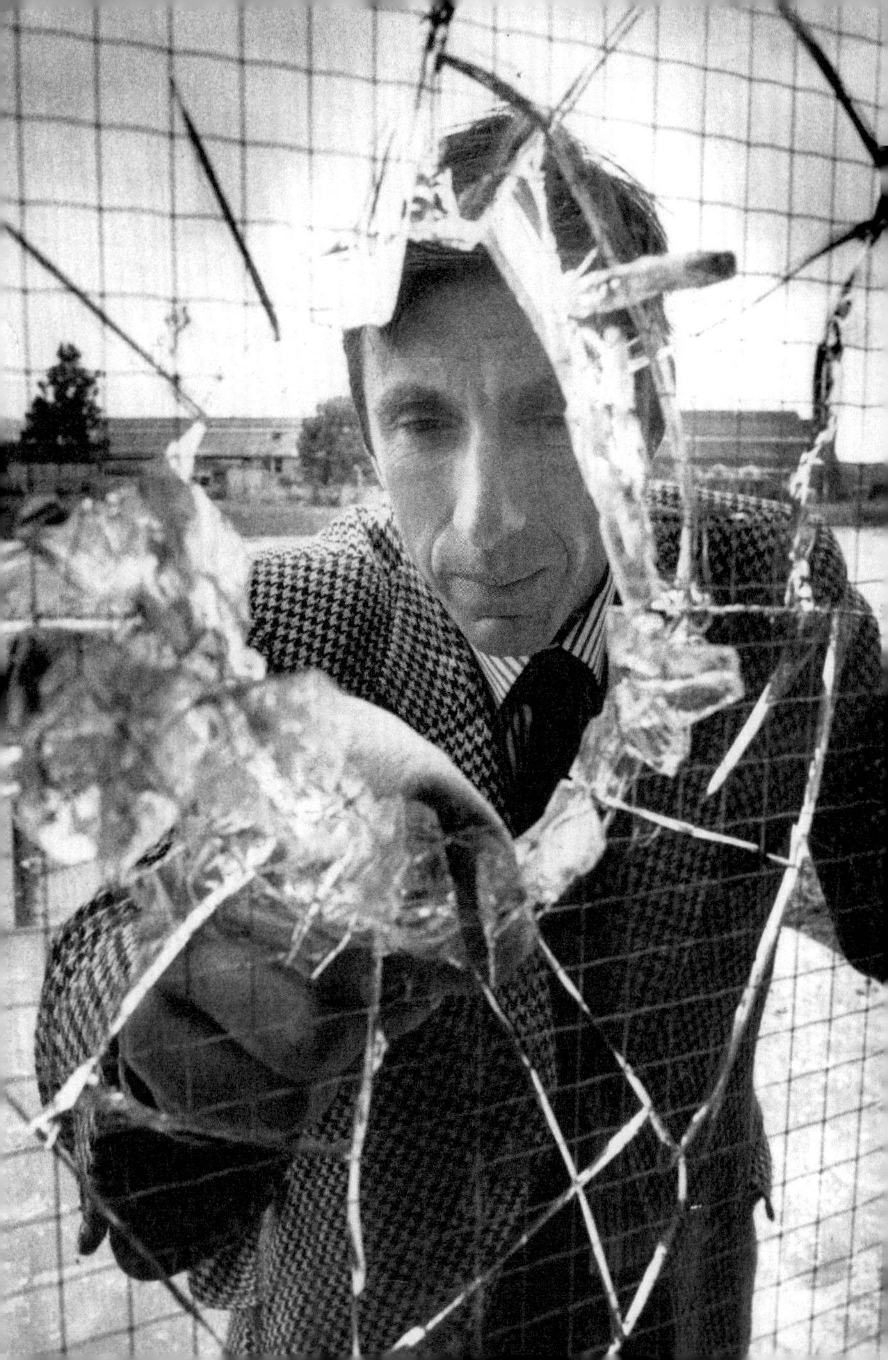

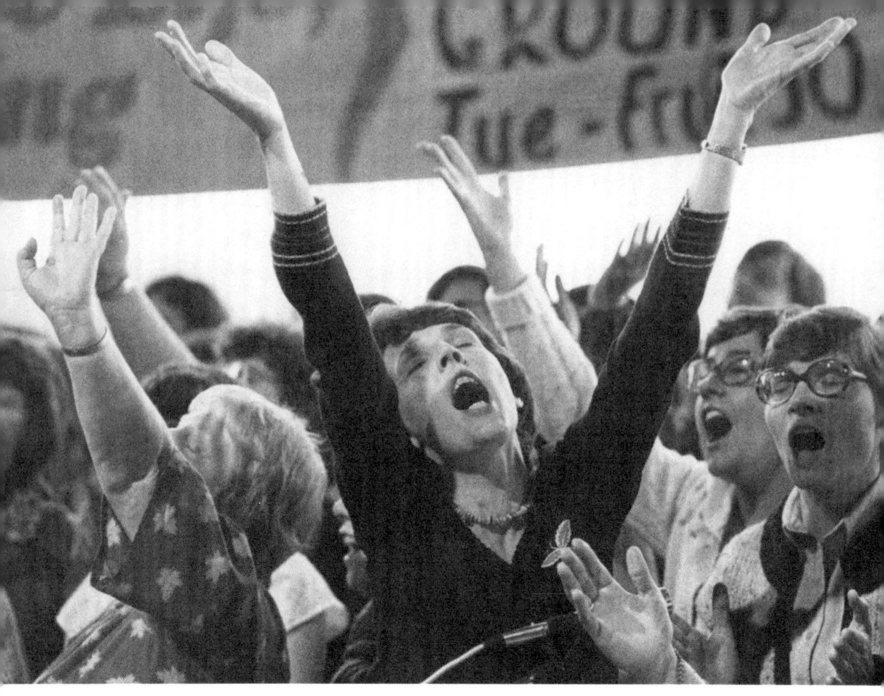

The ecstasy of the revelation
overcomes some devotees.

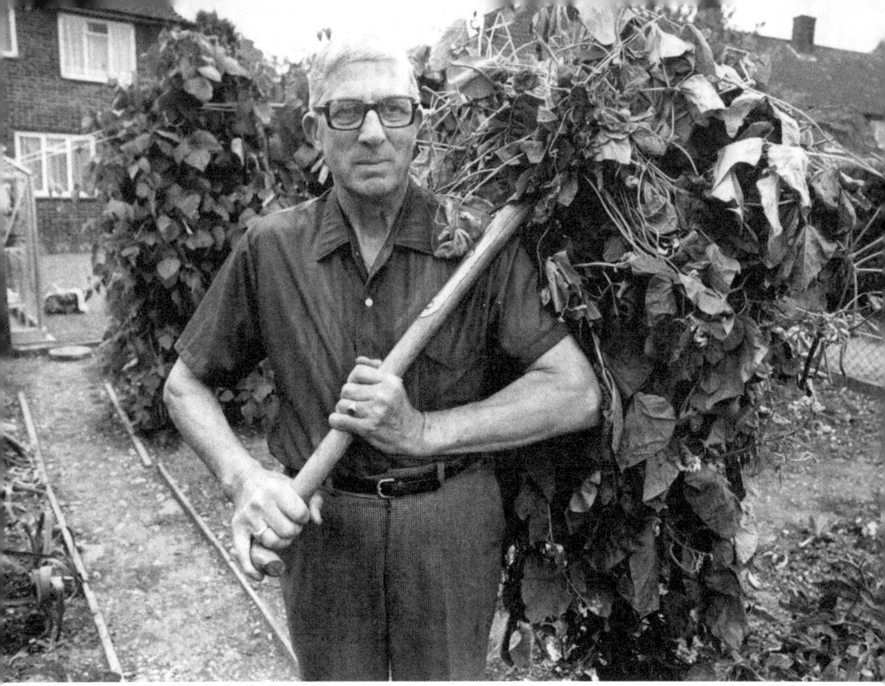

Bean mutations, Hayling Road,
South Oxhey.

An Army theatre group opening night. Their new production of “The Rain Willed It So” thrilled the audience in Luton yesterday.

Elizabeth Frink assures councillors that totems are the answer.

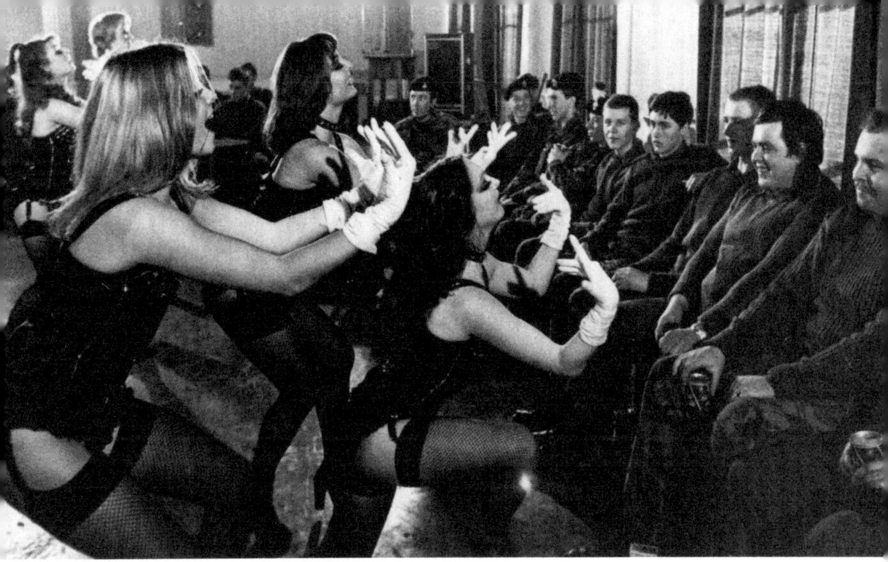

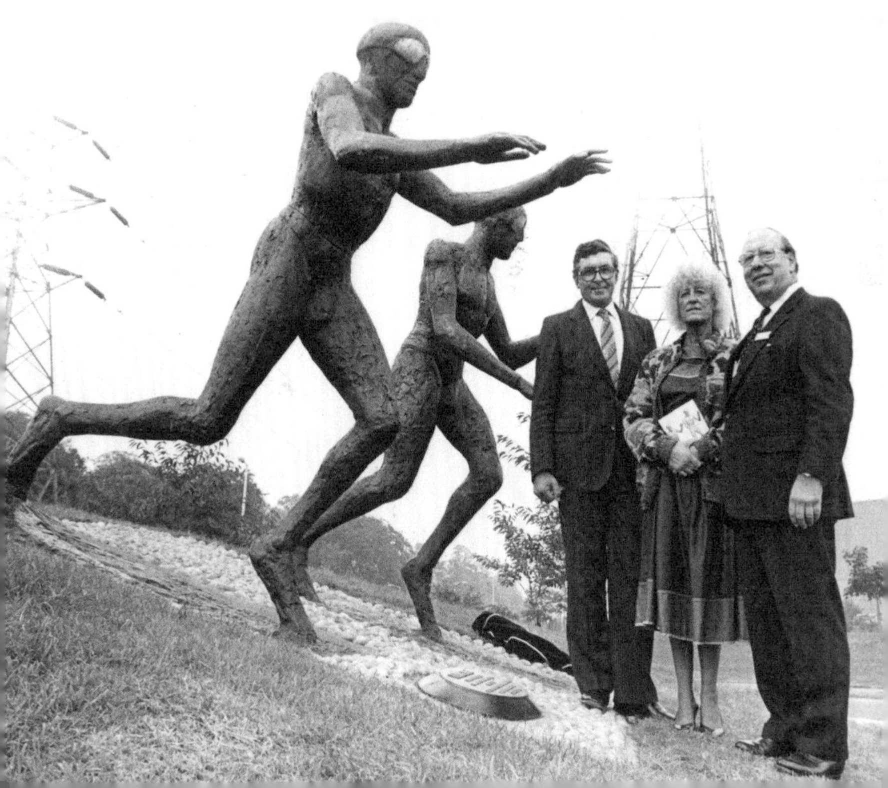

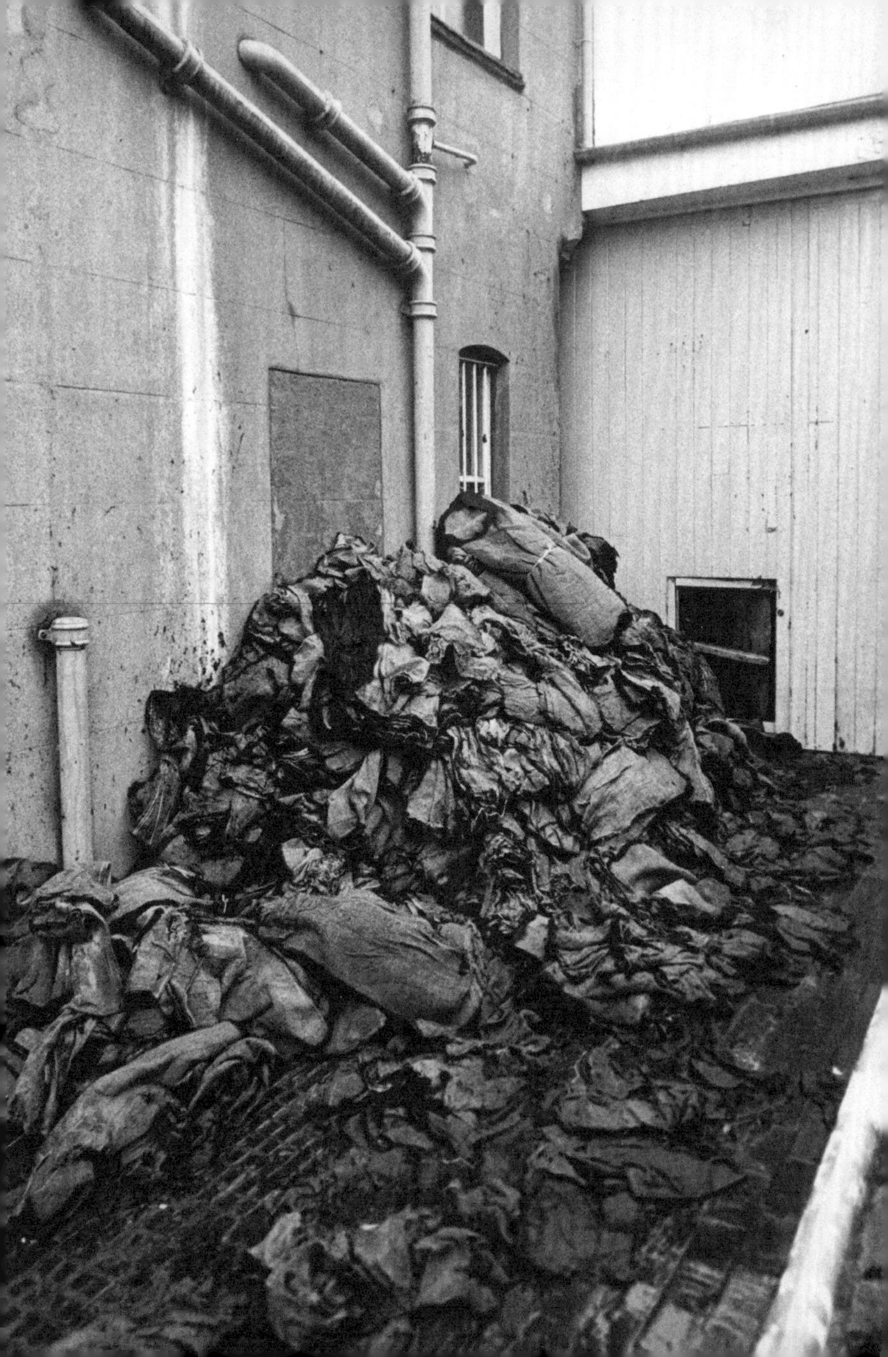

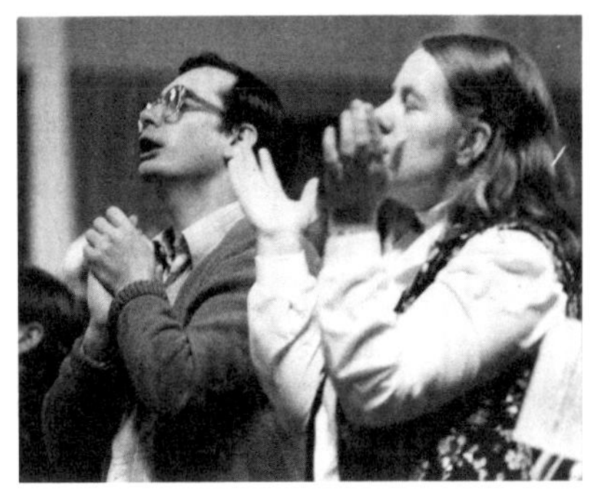

Followers at the Farley Hill apparition.

This apparition in Farley Hill does not auger well, but followers from across the world have flocked to worship.

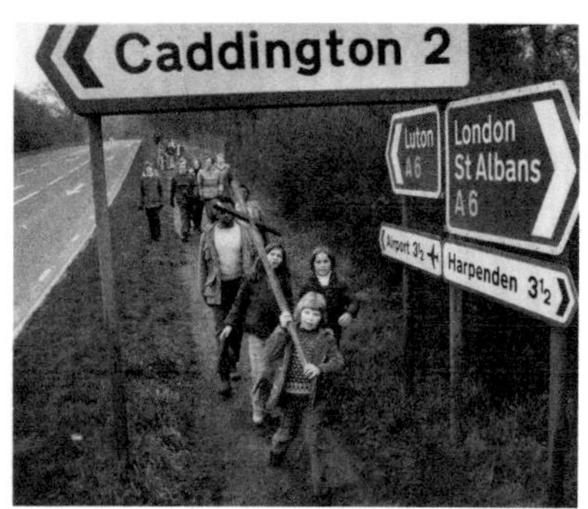

Spontaneous Calvary near Caddington.

Clifford and the shattered glass at Hookers Court, Luton.

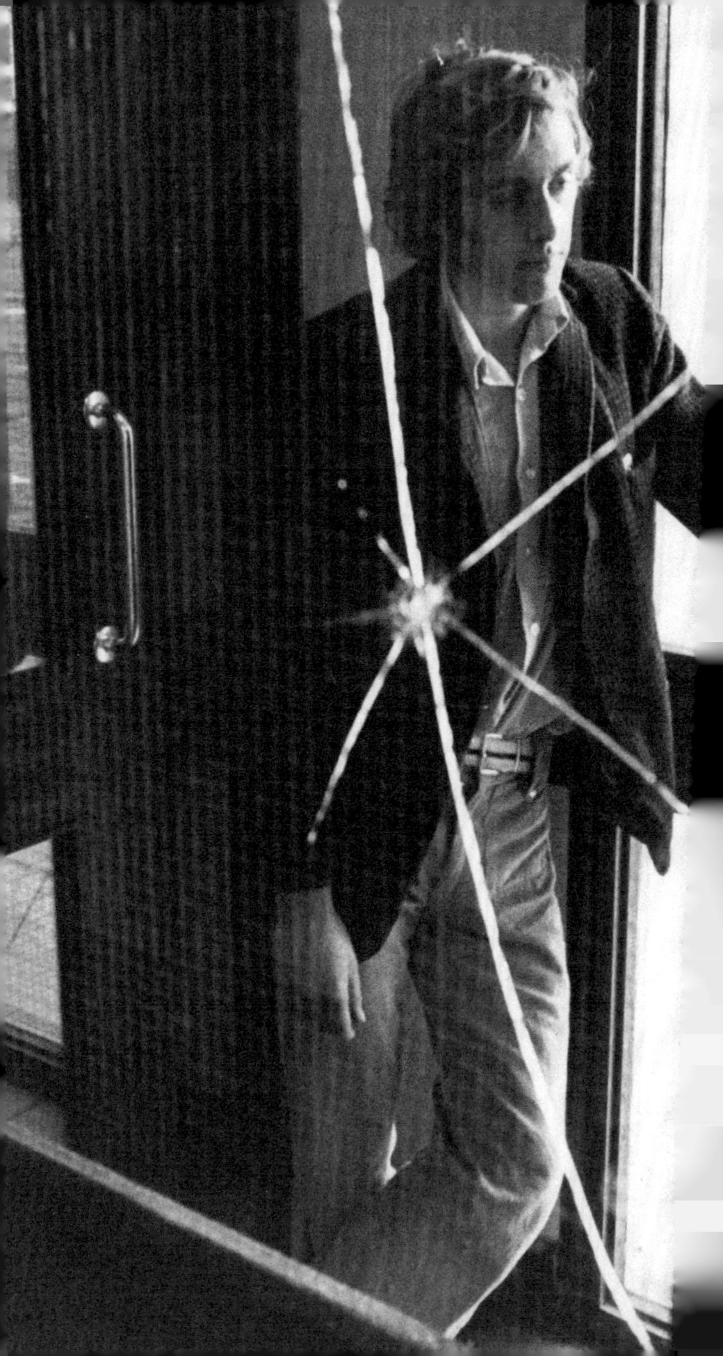

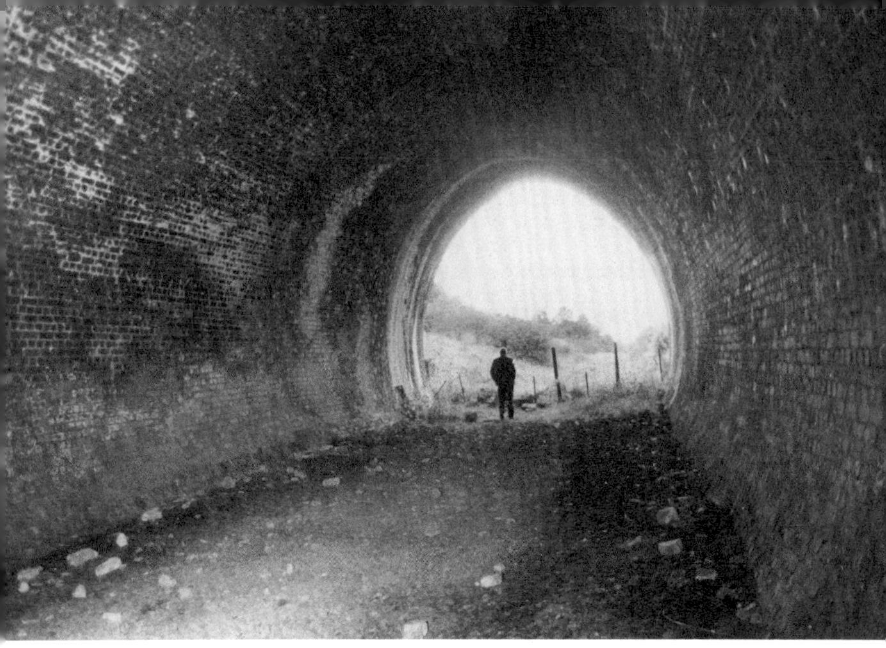

Tunnels of all kinds have been
sanctified. This example
at South Hill Park has been
cordoned off.
Inappropriate rituals were
taking place daily.

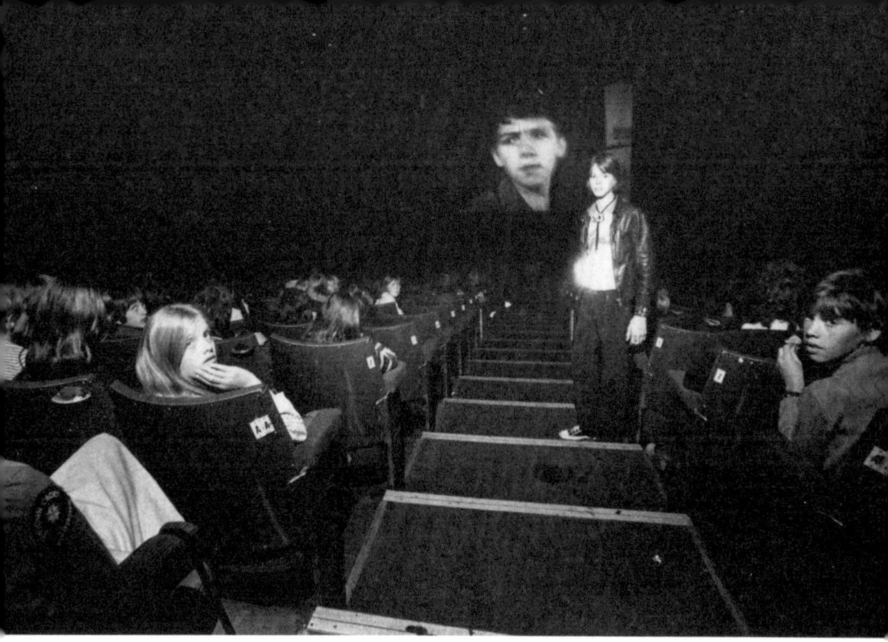

An afternoon at the cinema, Borehamwood. Important films about the coming and related matters are broadcast before and after the main feature. Flood drills are as important as the emphasis on spiritual preparation.

Shoe-changing protests have erupted in every high street.

Water damage to the parquet floor at Herts Art College.
Mr Pryde was first witness.

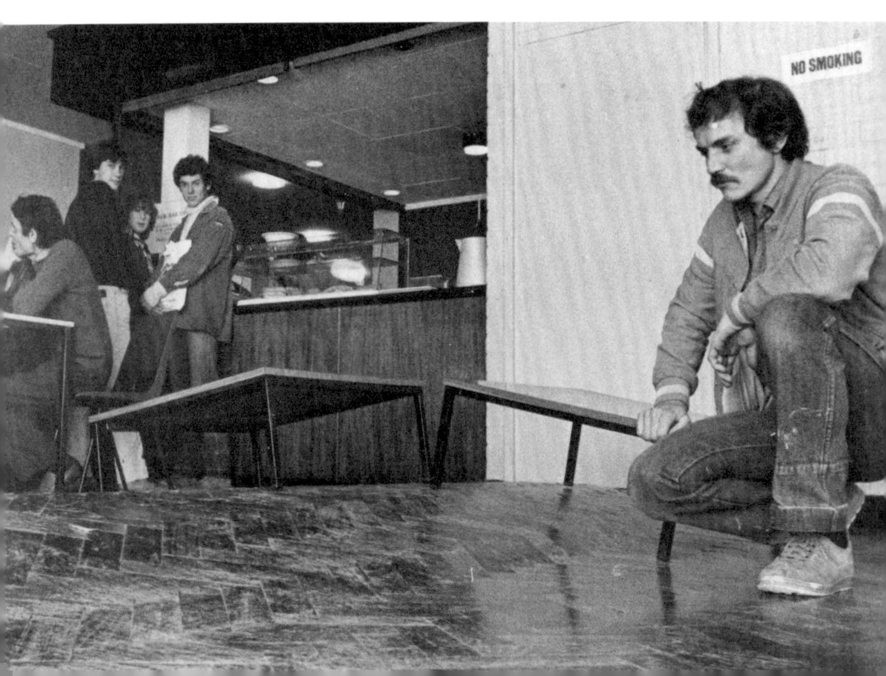

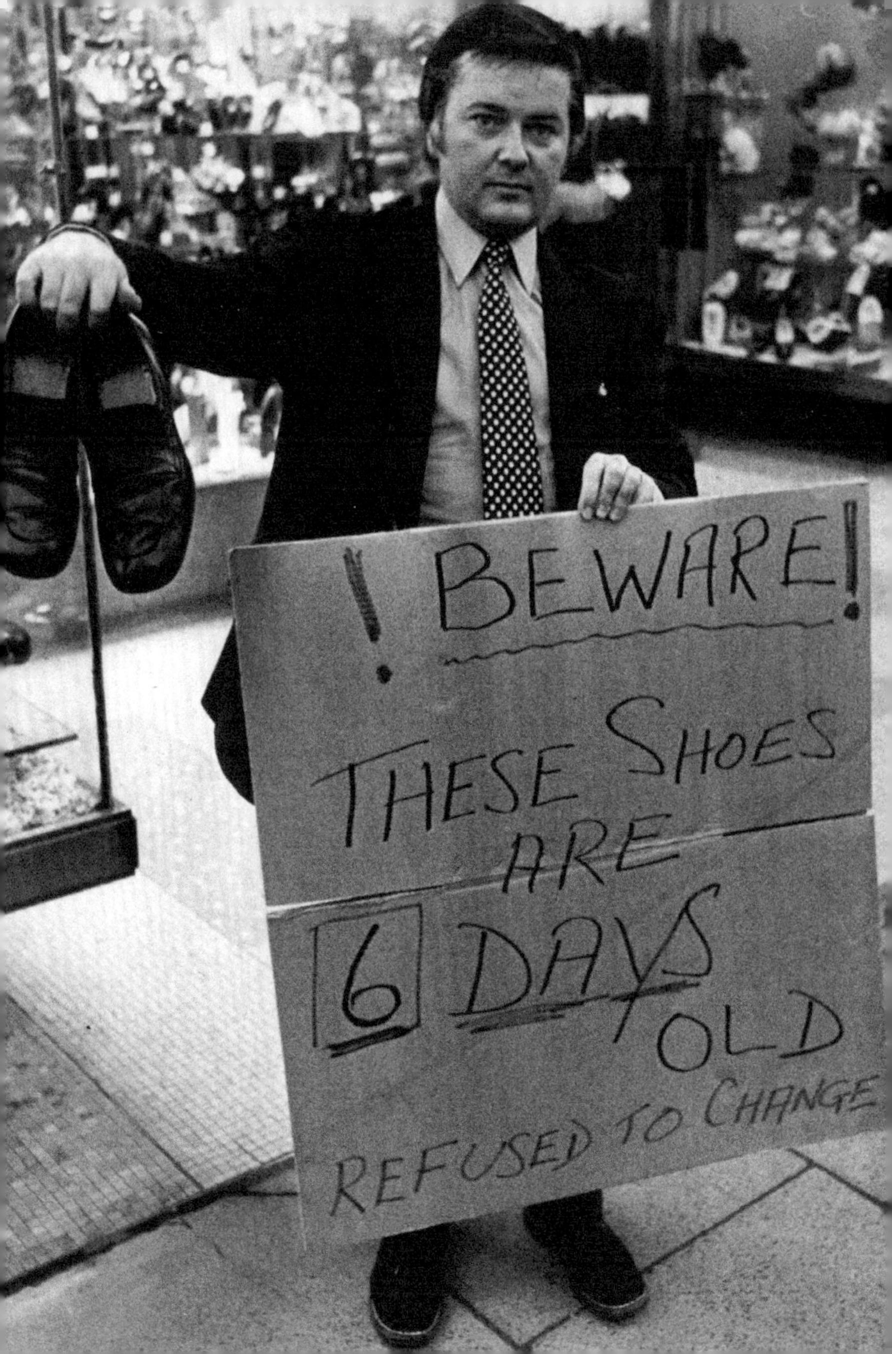
! BEWARE !
THESE SHOES ARE
6 DAYS OLD
REFUSED TO CHANGE

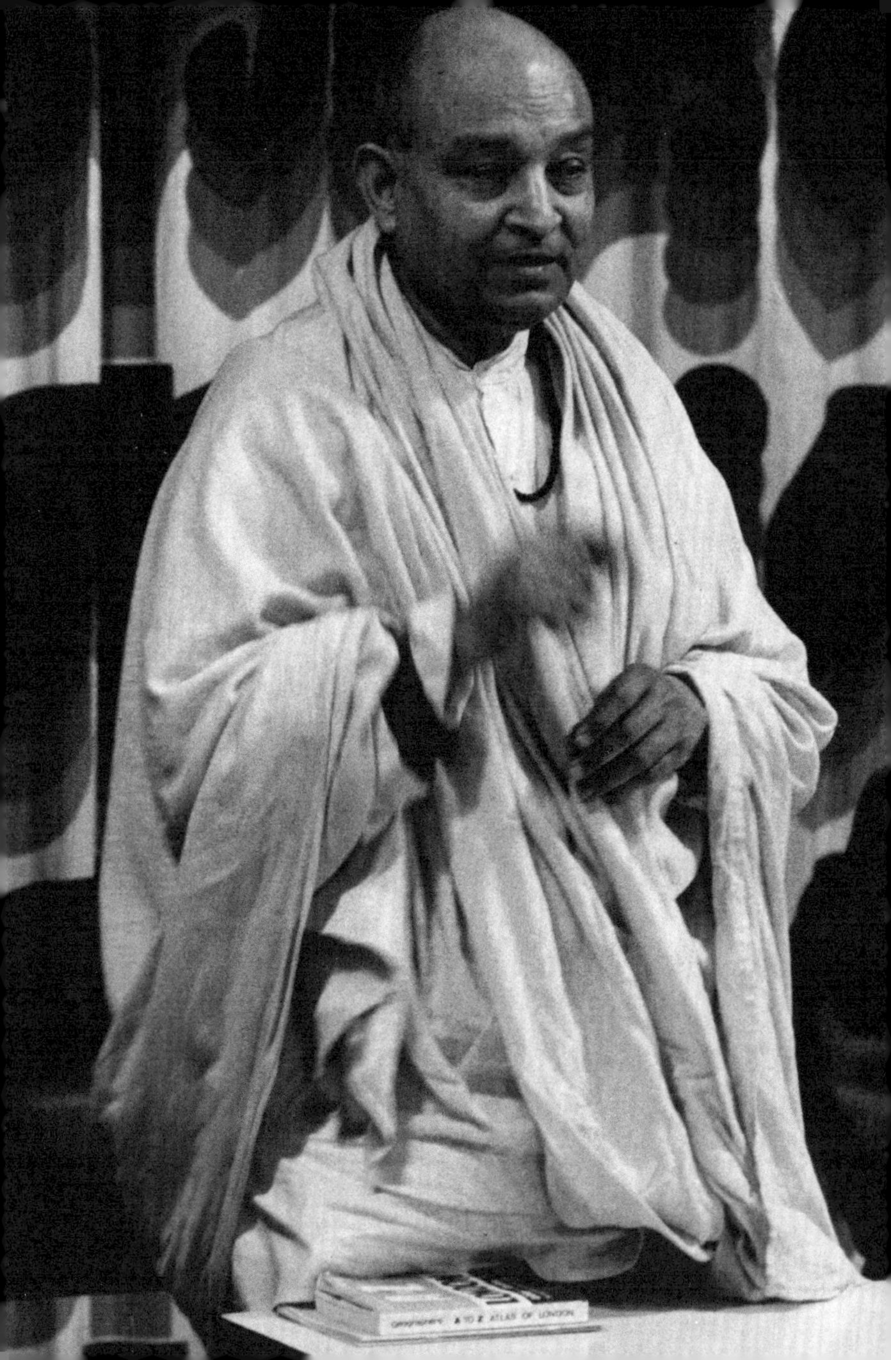
A TO Z ATLAS OF LONDON

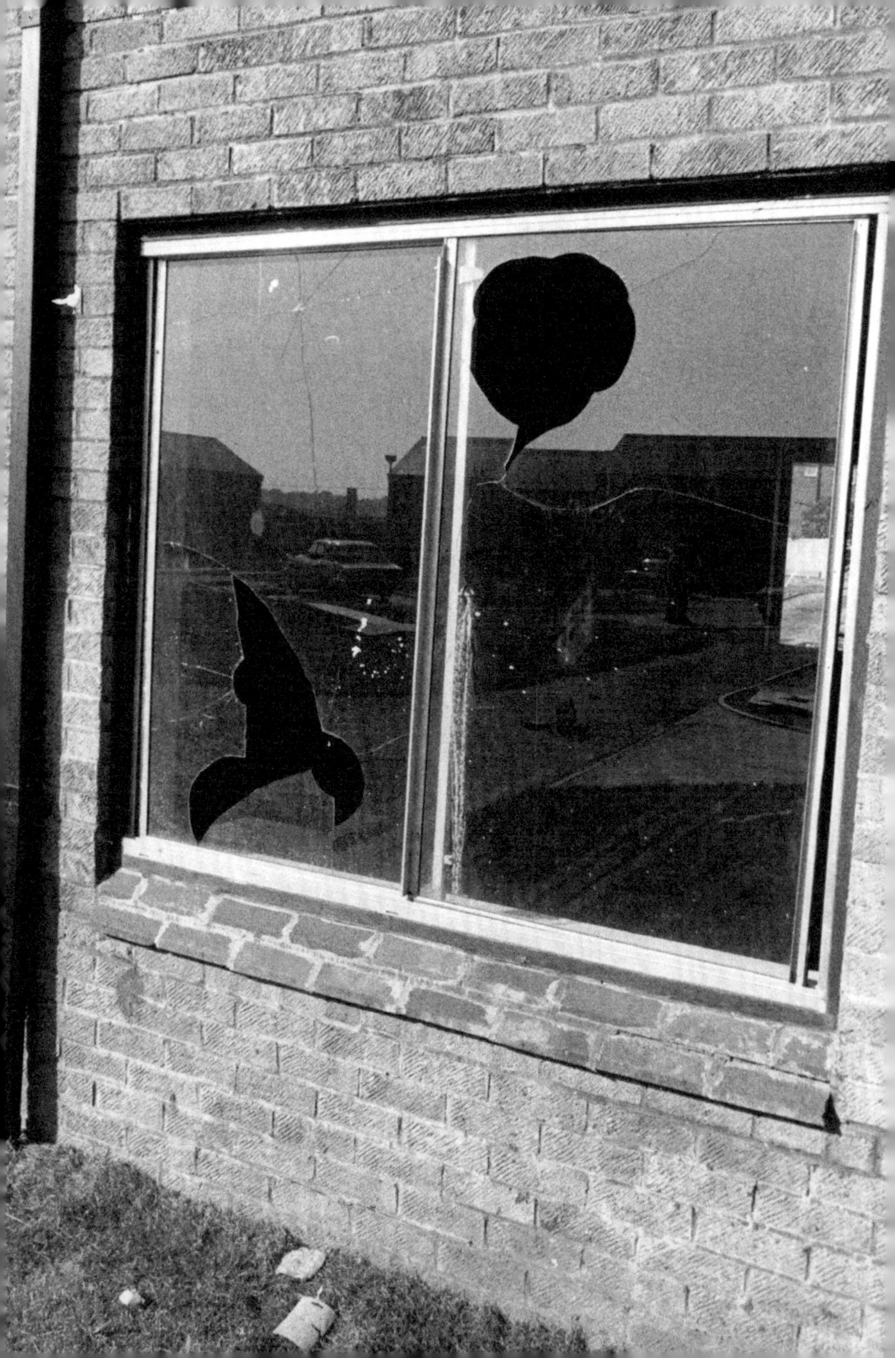

Swami Radananda answers questions about the nature of broken glass at Borehamwood College of Further Education last Monday night.

Broken window mystery, Dunstable

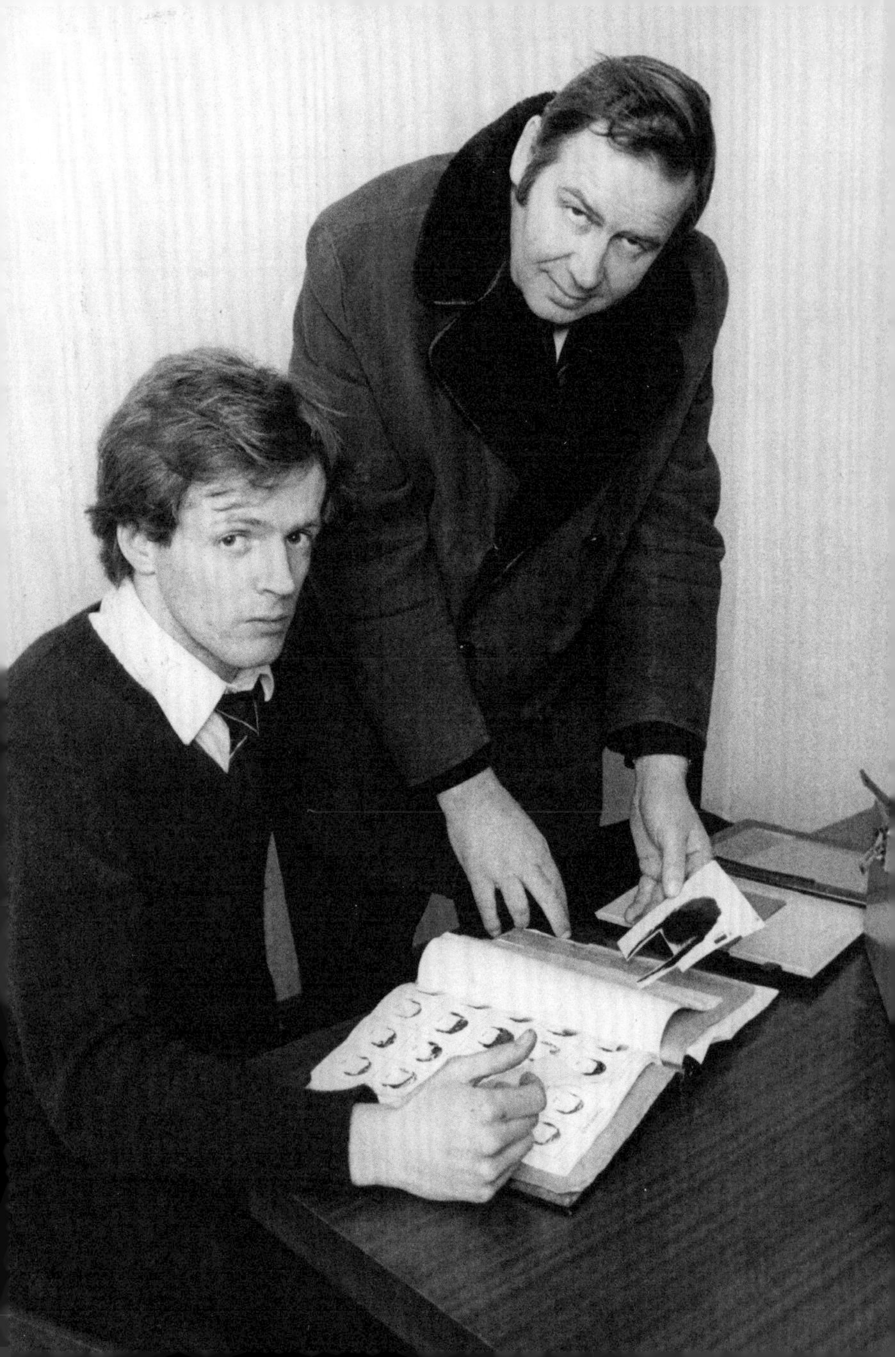

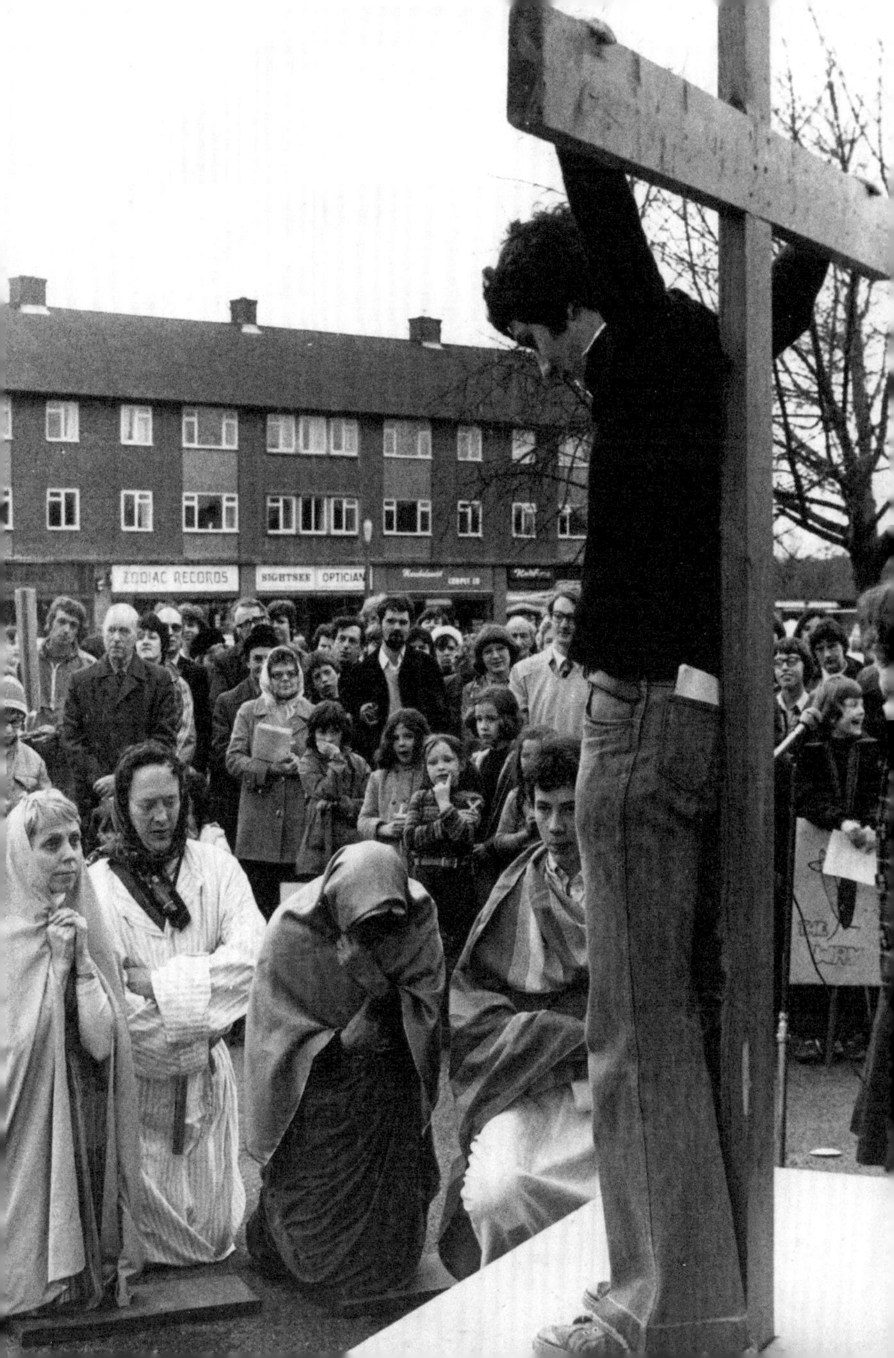
ZODIAC RECORDS
SIGHTSEE OPTICIAN

Luton police believe they have identified the Messiah.

He is crucified.

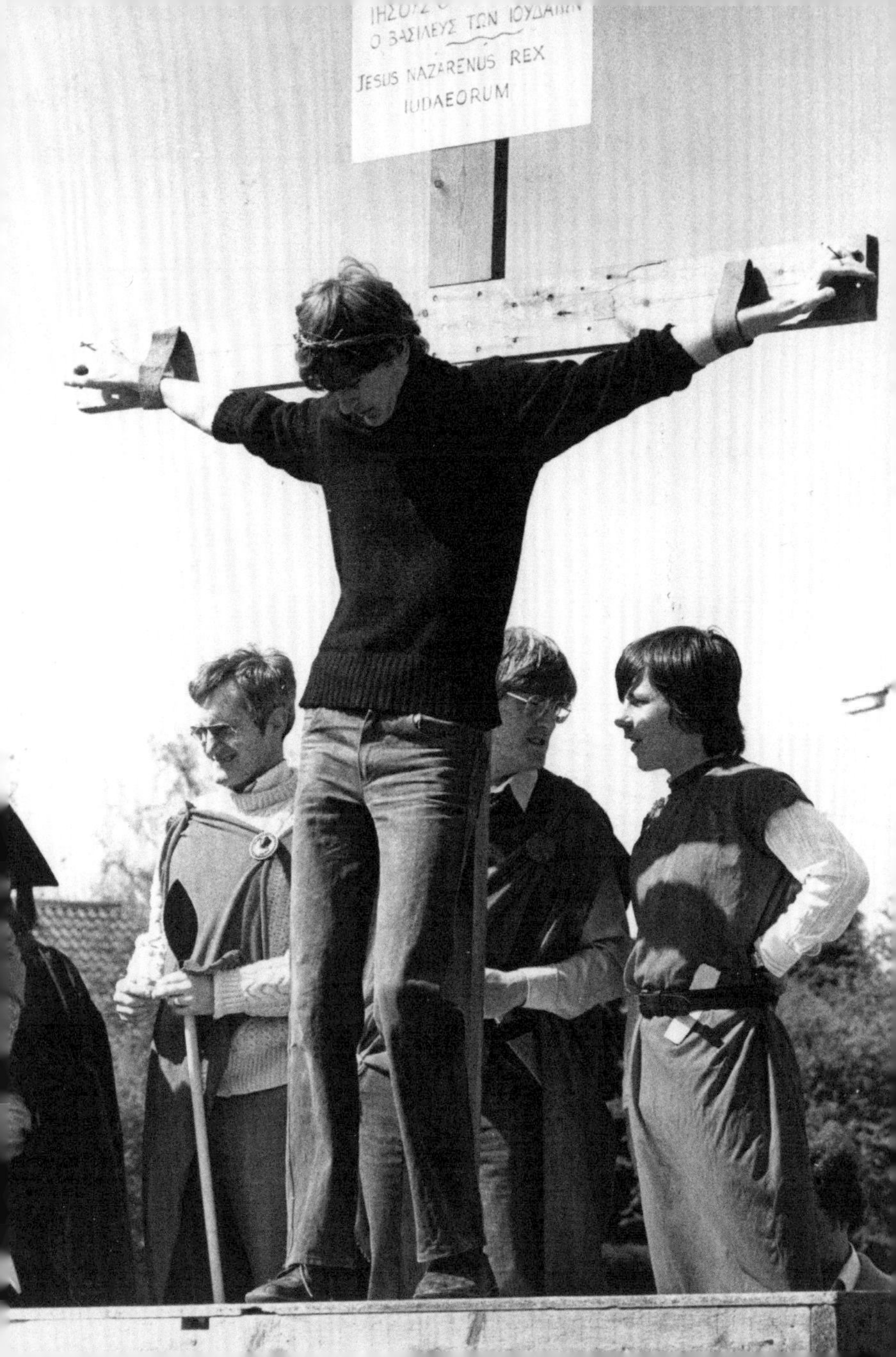
Ο ΒΑΣΙΛΕΥΣ ΤΩΝ ΙΟΥΔΑΙΩΝ
JESUS NAZARENUS REX
IUDAEORUM

Rex.

The King appears at Queensway Hall, Dunstable.

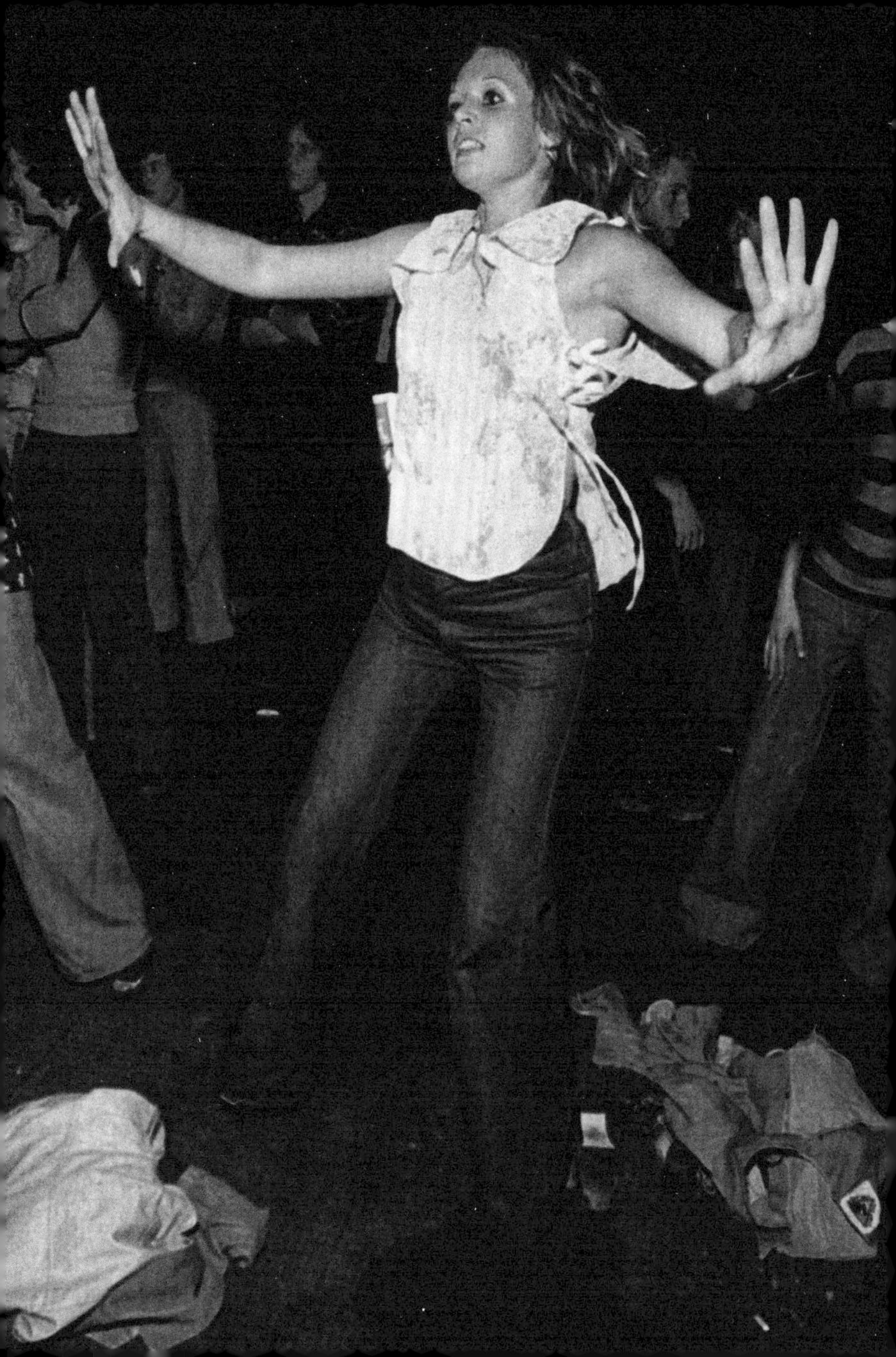

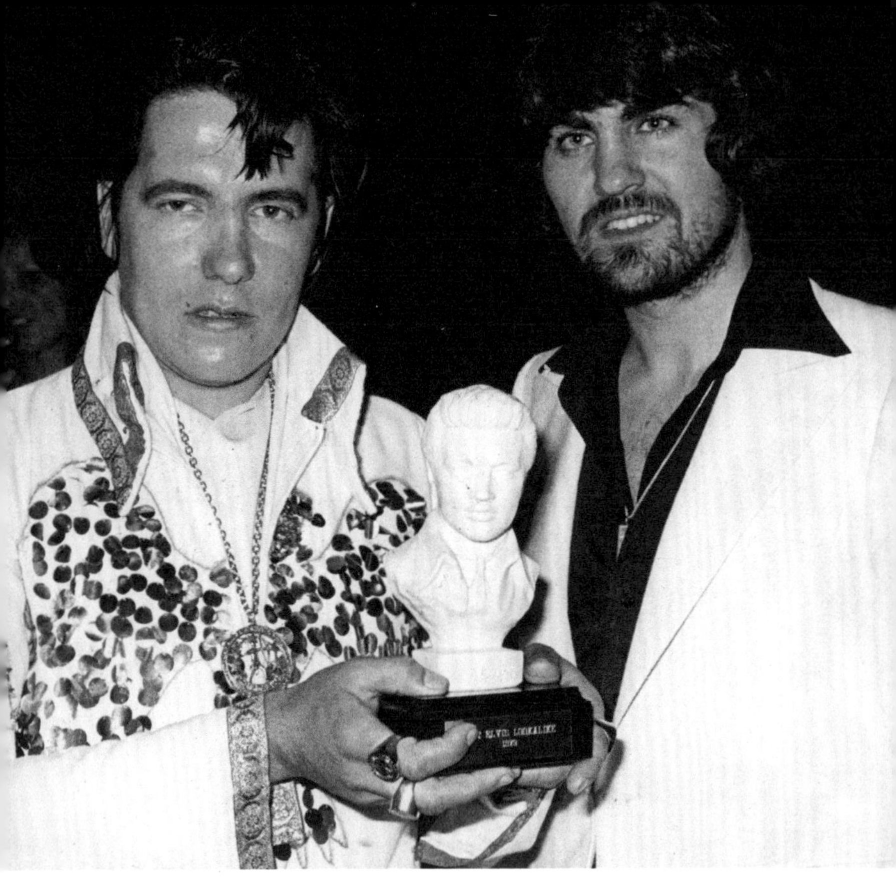

The King in Watford with disciple.

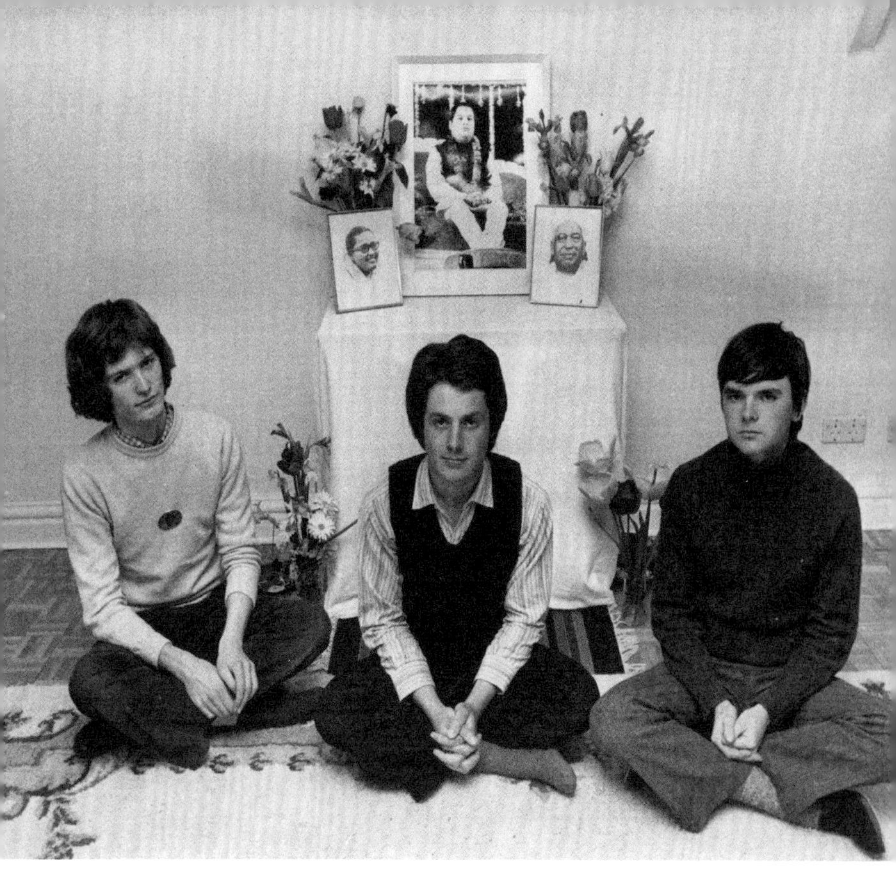

New Followers, Hemel Hempstead.

The King disappears in the
blighted earth. Hope springs
eternal. Where is the King?

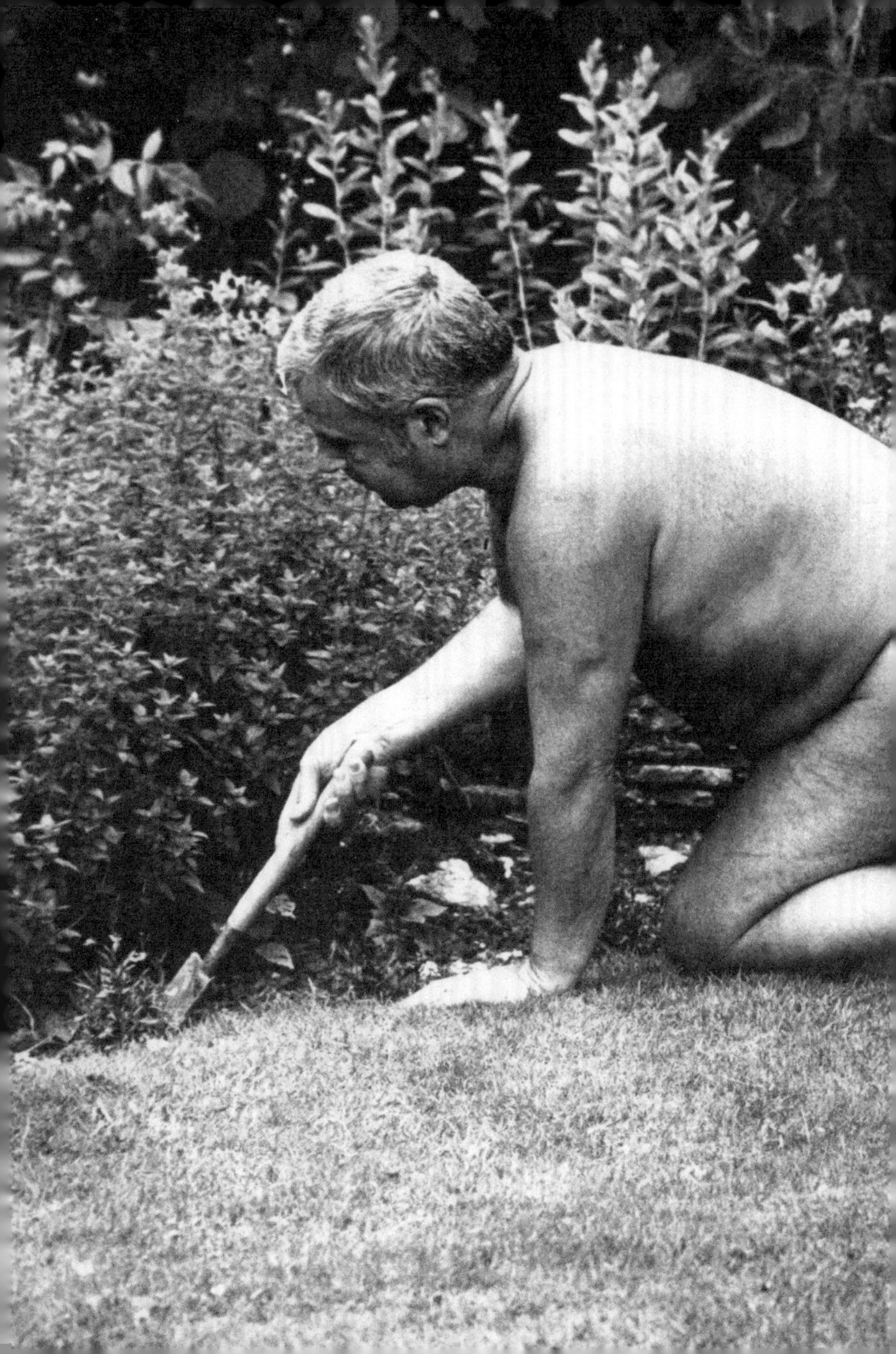

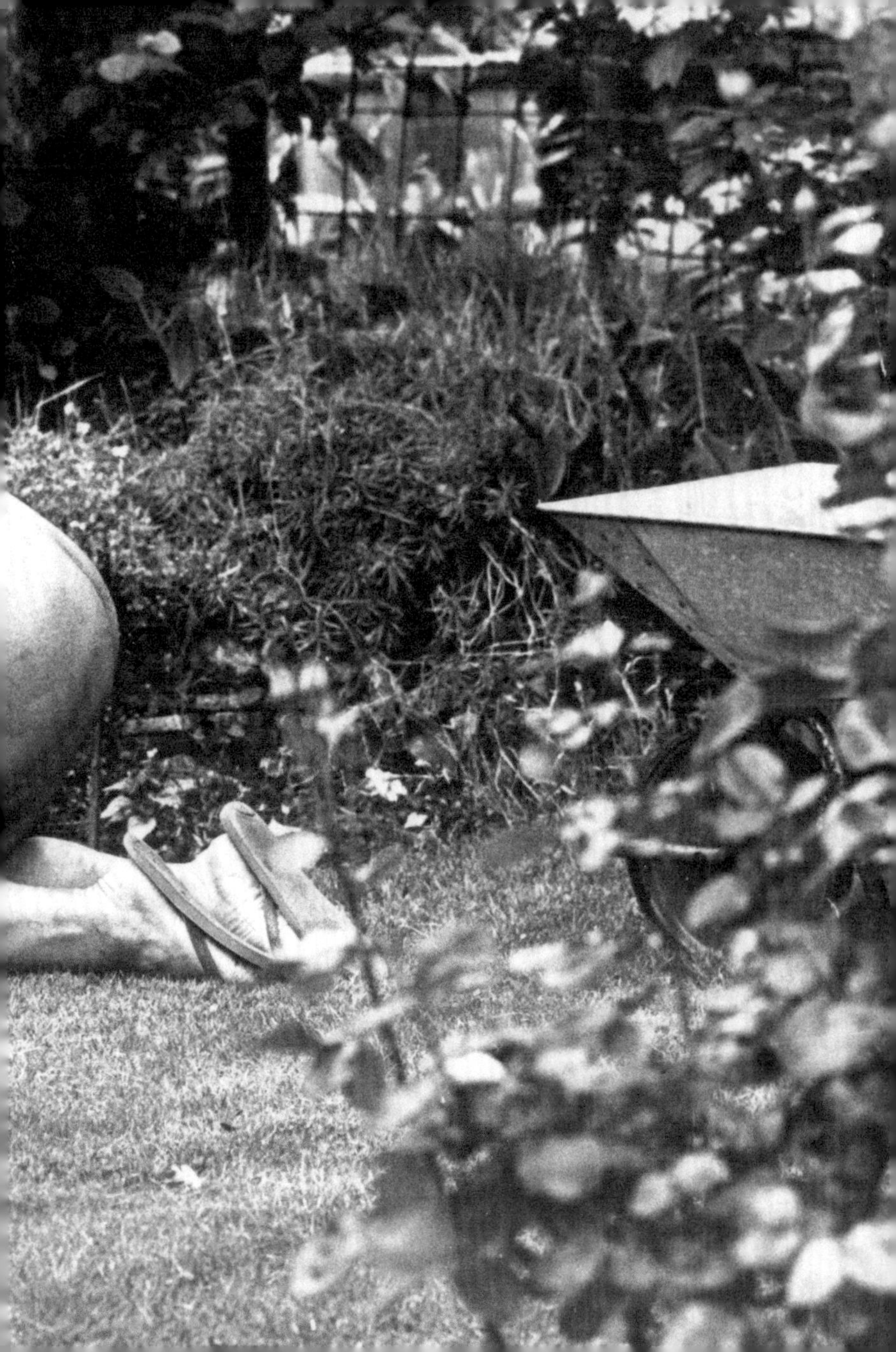

The search for the Chosen One
is performed in every garden,
in every street. The will of
the people is now united.
No stone is left unturned.

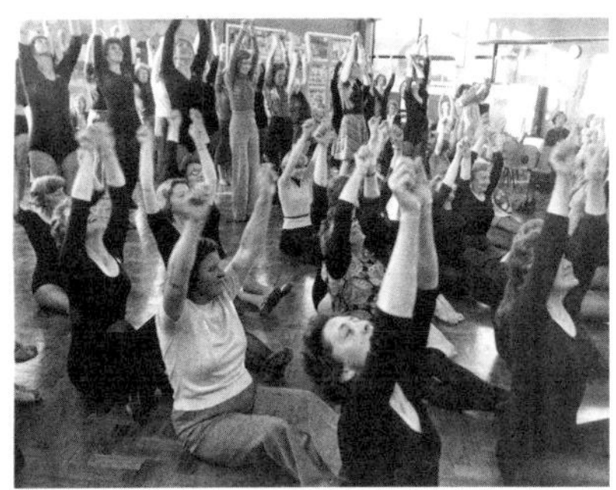

Months have passed since the Messiah disappeared.
In Croxley Green on Wednesday a wave of hope washed over a community gathering.

He is found in the Schweppes car park in Aylesbury. The search is over. A new world has dawned.

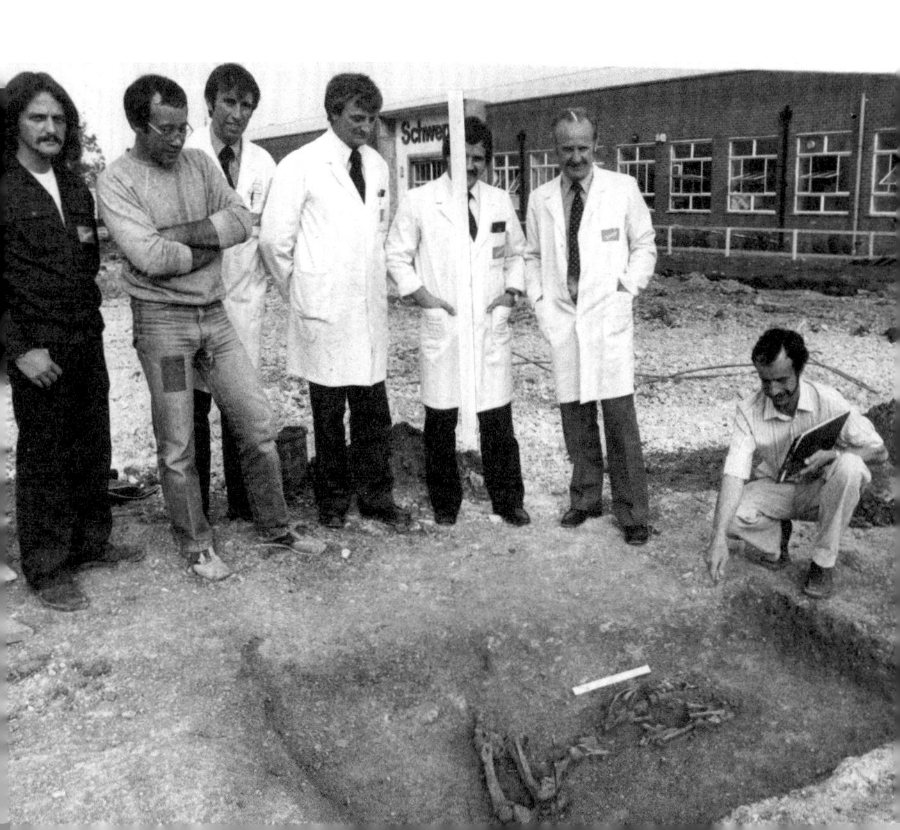

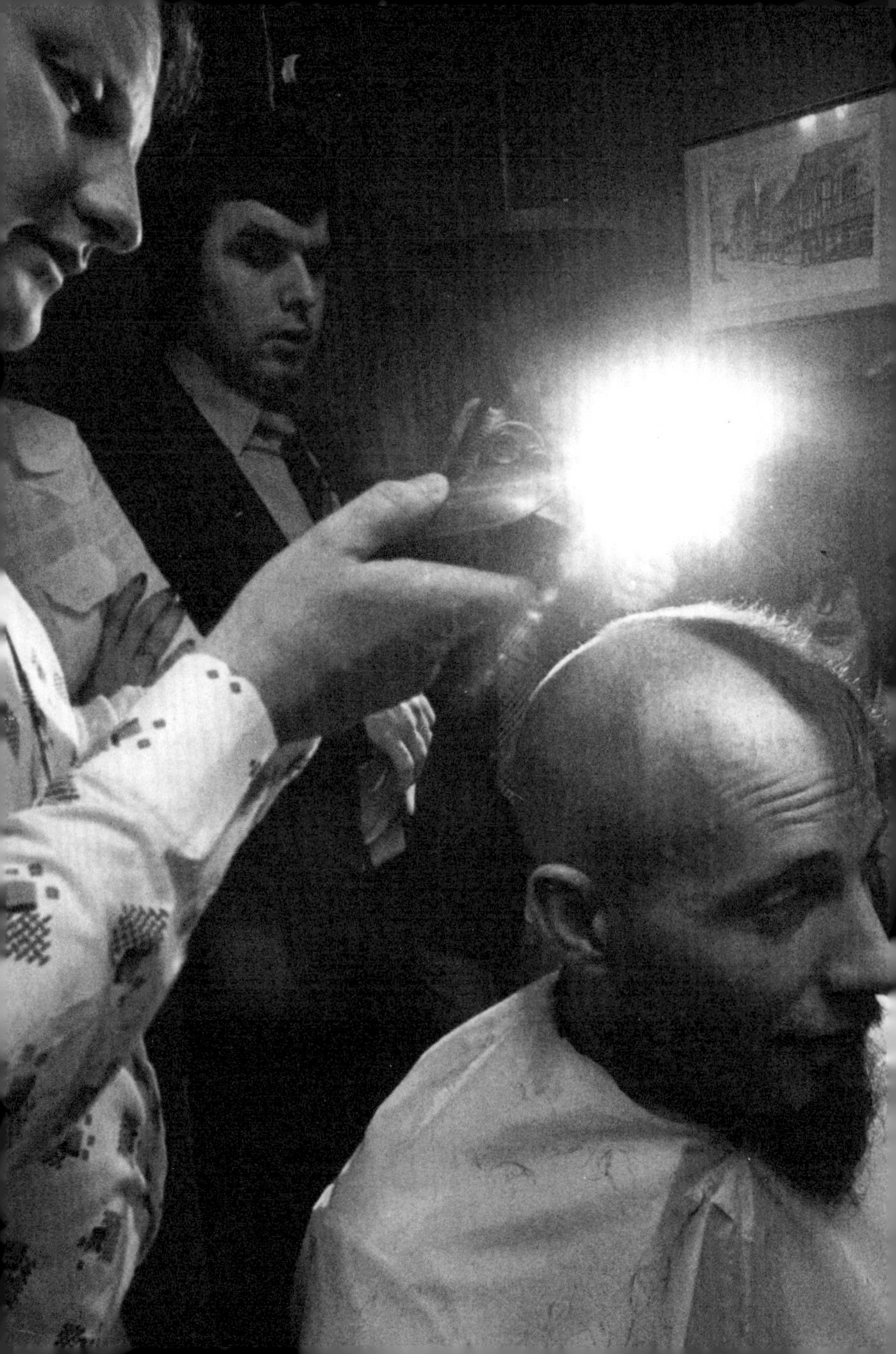

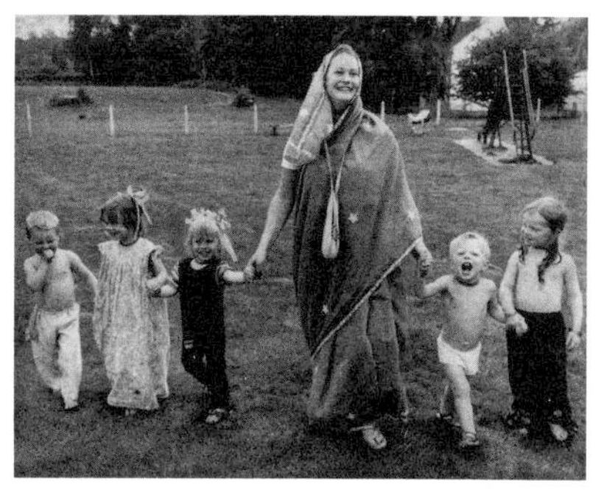

Letchmore Heath, Elysian Fields.

A mass shaving of heads occurs as the news of the King spreads through the shires. In this picture Dick Burden reveals the scalp of an adherent in Hitchin.

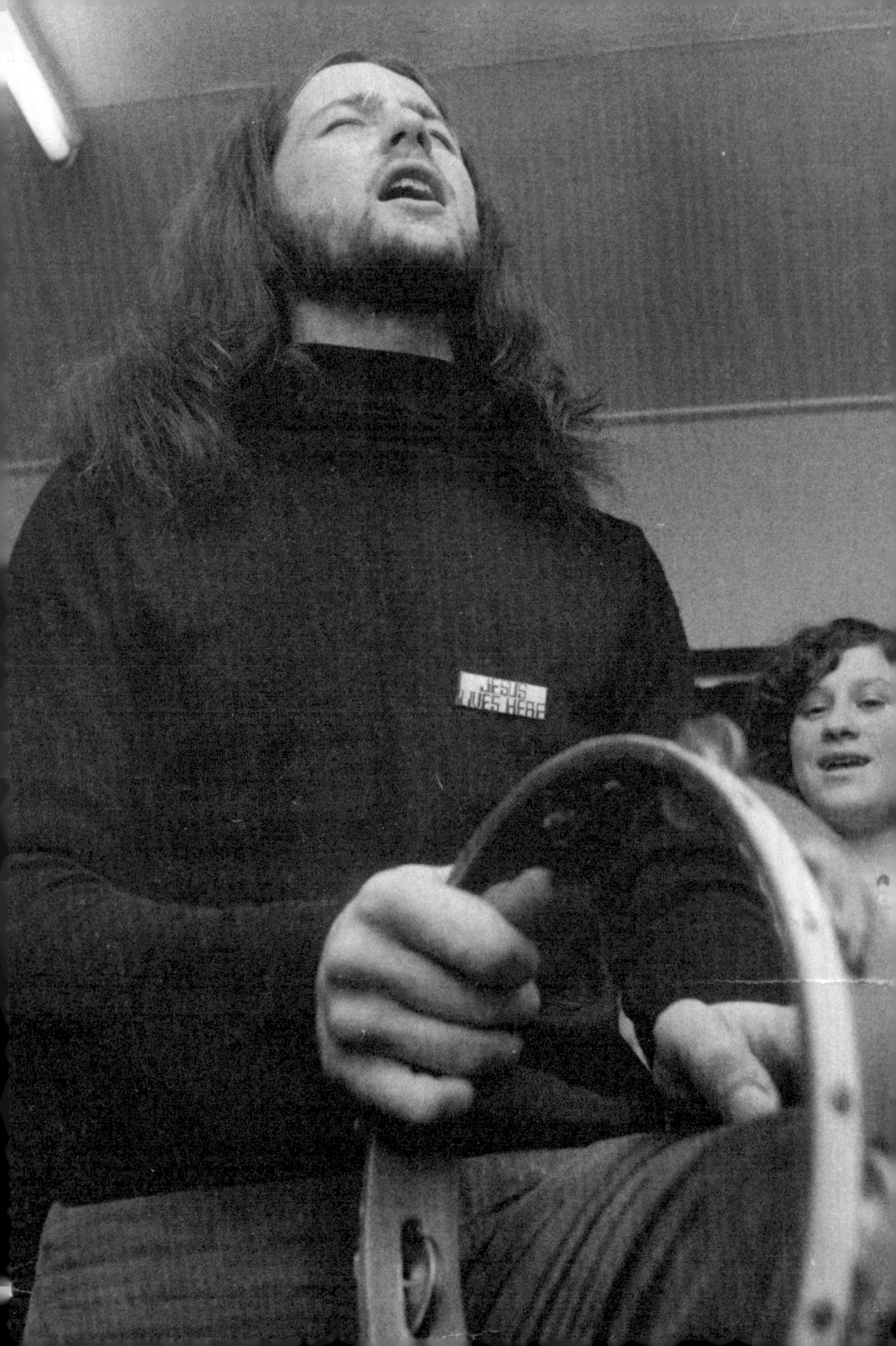
JESUS
HERE

The crisis is over. Celebrations rock the nation.

Lucy Preston discovers the source of the holy water in Radlett.

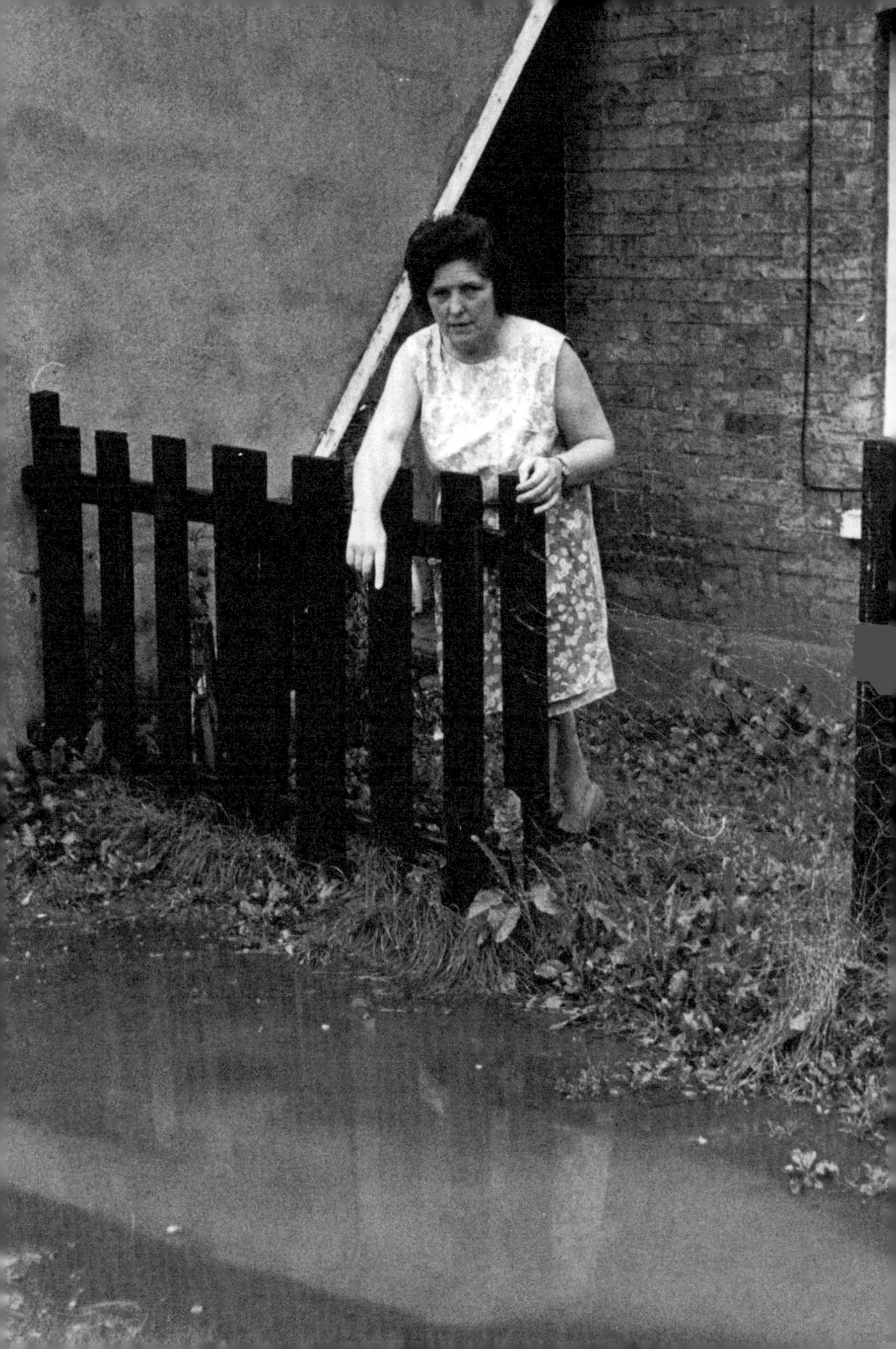

Concept and texts
Timothy Prus

All photographs courtesy of the
AMC Collection

Publisher
RVB BOOKS
Matthieu Charon & Rémi Faucheux

Conception & graphic design
Zoé Aubry

ISBN
979-10-90306-62-2

Achevé d'imprimer en
mai 2017

Dépôt légal
mai 2017